**Editor**
Eric Migliaccio

**Managing Editor**
Ina Massler Levin, M.A.

**Illustrator**
Renée Christine Yates

**Cover Artist**
Brenda DiAntonis

**Art Coordinator**
Kevin Barnes

**Imaging**
Ralph Olmedo, Jr.
James Edward Grace

**Publisher**
Mary Dupuy Smith, M.S. Ed.

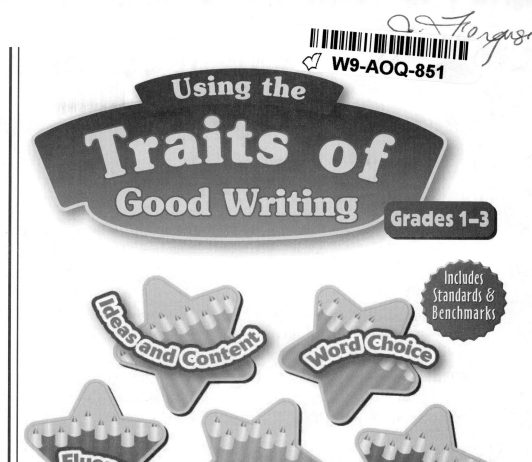

# Using the Traits of Good Writing

**Grades 1–3**

Includes Standards & Benchmarks

Ideas and Content

Word Choice

Fluency

Voice

Organization

Conventions

Presentation

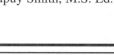

**Author**

Tracie Heskett

***Teacher Created Resources, Inc.***
6421 Industry Way
Westminster, CA 92683
www.teachercreated.com

**ISBN: 978-0-7439-3276-9**

©*2002 Teacher Created Resources, Inc.*
Reprinted, 2008
Made in U.S.A.

# Table of Contents

# Introduction

## ➤ What Is Trait Writing?

In the early 1980s, teachers in the northwestern United States felt they needed a set of common guidelines by which to teach and assess student writing. By comparing student writing that needed extensive revision to student writing that did not, certain characteristics—or traits—emerged. The qualities found in successful student writing have been revised over time to form what is now known as "Six-Trait Writing." Recently, a seventh trait has been added, in keeping with current academic standards that include communication skills. Northwest Regional Educational Laboratories in Portland, Oregon, has been instrumental in defining and developing the traits and making workshops and other resources available to teachers.

These are the analytic traits identified for use in instructing and assessing student writing:

☆ **Ideas and Content** (page 6)        ☆ **Organization** (page 50)

☆ **Word Choice** (page 19)              ☆ **Conventions** (page 64)

☆ **Fluency** (page 28)                  ☆ **Presentation** (page 79)

☆ **Voice** (page 39)

For a definition of each trait, refer to the corresponding first page of each section in this book.

## ➤ Why Should I Teach Trait Writing?

The traits of good writing allows teachers and students to focus on one element of writing at a time, thus breaking the task of learning to write effectively into manageable parts.

Current academic standards refer to these qualities—voice, word choice, conventions, presentation, and communication—specifically. The traits apply to a variety of writing styles and purposes. Mastery of these traits goes beyond simply "teaching to the test" and gives students skills they can use for life.

## ➤ How Do I Teach the Traits in the Classroom?

One trait can be taught each week for seven weeks; there are daily lessons for each of the traits. A teacher may also teach one entire trait on a single day as a more comprehensive thematic unit. Lessons should be taught in the order given, as many lessons build on material previously covered and/or exercises already completed. Have students write in a writing notebook or save their writing in a folder for future use. When completing the writing exercises, students should skip a line in their writing or double space; these rough drafts will be used in later lessons to provide editing practice.

Each trait includes a literature-based lesson, which introduces students to writing exhibiting one or more of the traits. Each lesson incorporates one or more academic standards. These standards are from *Content Knowledge: A Compendium of Standards and Benchmarks for K–12 Education* (Second Edition, 1997) synthesized by John S. Kendall and Robert J. Marzano. The book is published jointly by McREL (Mid-continent Regional Educational Laboratory, Inc.) and ASCD (Association for Supervision and Curriculum Development). Used by permission of McREL.

# Standards for Writing

The following standards are used by permission of McREL (Copyright 2000 McREL, Mid-continent Research for Education and Learning. Telephone: 303-337-0990. Website: www.mcrel.org)

**1. Demonstrates competence in the general skills and strategies of the writing process**

**A. Prewriting:** Uses prewriting strategies to plan written work (e.g., discusses ideas with peers, draws pictures to generate ideas, writes key thoughts and questions, rehearses ideas, records reactions and observations)

**B.** Uses graphic organizers, story maps, and webs; groups related ideas; takes notes; brainstorms ideas

**C. Drafting and Revising:** Uses strategies to draft and revise written work (e.g., rereads; rearranges words, sentences, and paragraphs to improve or clarify meaning; varies sentence type; adds descriptive words and details; deletes extraneous information; incorporates suggestions from peers and teachers; sharpens the focus)

**D.** Elaborates on a central idea; uses paragraphs to develop separate ideas

**E. Editing and Publishing:** Uses strategies to edit and publish written work (e.g., proofreads using a dictionary and other resources; edits for grammar, punctuation, capitalization, and spelling at a developmentally appropriate level; incorporates illustrations or photos; shares finished product)

**F.** Evaluates own and others' writing (e.g., asks questions and makes comments about writing, helps classmates apply grammatical and mechanical conventions)

**G.** Dictates or writes with a logical sequence of events (e.g., includes a beginning, middle, and ending)

**H.** Dictates or writes detailed descriptions of familiar persons, places, objects, or experiences

**I.** Writes in response to literature

**J.** Writes in a variety of formats (e.g., picture books, letters, stories, poems, information pieces)

**K.** Writes expressive composition (e.g., expresses ideas, reflections, and observations; uses an individual, authentic voice; uses relevant details; and presents ideas that enable a reader to imagine the world of the event or experience)

**L.** Writes autobiographical compositions (e.g., provides a context within which the incident occurs, uses simple narrative strategies, provides some insight into why this incident is memorable)

# Standards for Writing (cont.)

2. **Develops awareness of the stylistic and rhetorical aspects of writing (i.e., sentence structure and rhythm)**

    **A.** Uses general, frequently used words to convey basic ideas

    **B.** Uses descriptive language that clarifies and enhances ideas (e.g., describes familiar people, places, or objects)

    **C.** Uses a variety of sentence structures

3. **Uses grammatical and mechanical conventions in written compositions**

4. **Gathers and uses information for research purposes**

    **A.** Generates questions about topics of personal interest

    **B.** Uses a variety of strategies to identify topics to investigate (e.g., brainstorms, lists questions, uses idea webs)

    **C.** Compiles information into oral reports

5. **Demonstrates competence in speaking and listening as tools for learning**

    **A.** Makes contributions in class and group discussions (e.g., recounts personal experiences, reports on personal knowledge about a topic, initiates conversations

    **B.** Asks and responds to questions

    **C.** Reads compositions to the class

    **D.** Organizes ideas for oral presentations (e.g., includes content appropriate to the audience, uses notes or other memory aids, summarizes main points)

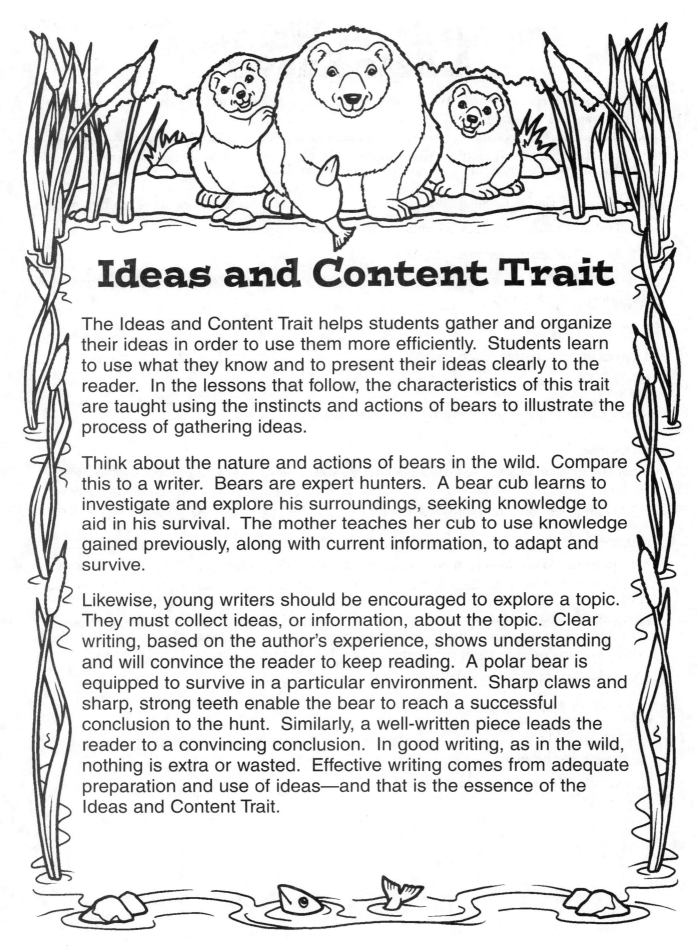

# Ideas and Content Trait

The Ideas and Content Trait helps students gather and organize their ideas in order to use them more efficiently. Students learn to use what they know and to present their ideas clearly to the reader. In the lessons that follow, the characteristics of this trait are taught using the instincts and actions of bears to illustrate the process of gathering ideas.

Think about the nature and actions of bears in the wild. Compare this to a writer. Bears are expert hunters. A bear cub learns to investigate and explore his surroundings, seeking knowledge to aid in his survival. The mother teaches her cub to use knowledge gained previously, along with current information, to adapt and survive.

Likewise, young writers should be encouraged to explore a topic. They must collect ideas, or information, about the topic. Clear writing, based on the author's experience, shows understanding and will convince the reader to keep reading. A polar bear is equipped to survive in a particular environment. Sharp claws and sharp, strong teeth enable the bear to reach a successful conclusion to the hunt. Similarly, a well-written piece leads the reader to a convincing conclusion. In good writing, as in the wild, nothing is extra or wasted. Effective writing comes from adequate preparation and use of ideas—and that is the essence of the Ideas and Content Trait.

# A Bear Knows

**Objective**

Given an introduction to the nature of bears and an overview of the characteristics of the Ideas and Content Trait, the student will employ one or more of the characteristics to generate a list of possible writing topics.

**Standards**

- Standard 4:  Gathers and uses information for research purposes
- Standard 4A:  Generates questions about topics of personal interest
- Standard 4B:  Uses a variety of strategies to identify topics to investigate (e.g., brainstorms, lists questions, uses idea webs)

**Materials**

- 2 copies of bear pattern (page 9)

**Preparation**

Enlarge two copies of the bear pattern for classroom display.

**Lesson Opening**

Show students the bear pattern.  Ask students how bears act.  Discuss the nature of bears:  they are excellent hunters, they explore and investigate their environment, they use their senses to gather information and reach a successful conclusion to the hunt, young cubs learn from their mothers, etc.

**Lesson Directions**

1. Ask students, "What do bears know a lot about?  What do you know a lot about?"  Tell students, "One aspect of writing is ideas, or what the author writes about."  Introduce the Ideas and Content Trait.  Suggest, "If I were to ask you to write about [this topic], would it be easy or hard?"  Compare the bear's nature and instincts to the Ideas and Content Trait.  Teach the specific characteristics of the trait, using the overhead, board, or other teaching aids.  Tell students their writing will have strong ideas and content when they do the following:

   - generate an intriguing topic
   - connect their writing to prior experience
   - use relevant, specific details
   - have clear ideas
   - surprise the reader with what they know

   Copy these characteristics onto one copy of the bear pattern.

# A Bear Knows *(cont.)*

**Lesson Directions** *(cont.)*

2. Discuss the characteristics. Tell students their writing will be more interesting to the reader if they write about what they know. Explain they may need to explore and investigate to learn more about their subject. Encourage students to collect information and/or write about their experiences. Tell them often, "A reader wants to know more. Show him or her what you know." Remind them to use examples and specific details.

3. Ask students, "Where do ideas come from?" Generate a class list on the second copy of the bear pattern or on chart paper. Title the poster "Where Do Ideas Come From?" and display it.

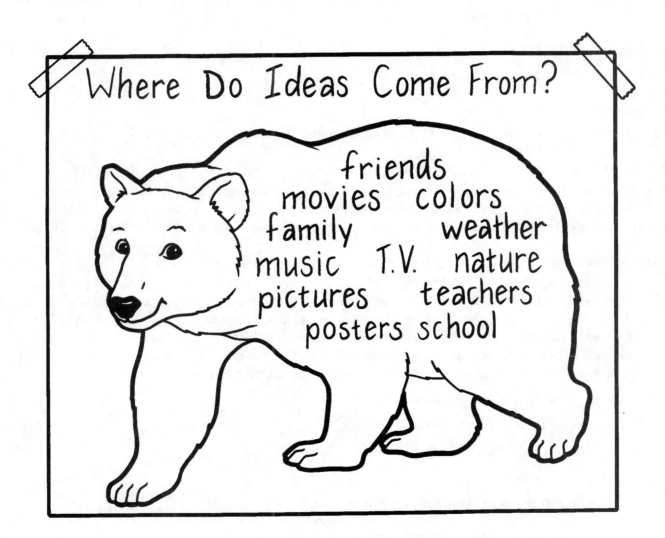

**Lesson Closing**

Ask students, "How will this trait help you in your writing? What do you think will be the hardest thing for you to do as you try to put this trait into practice in your own writing? What will be the easiest thing to remember?"

# Bear Pattern

# My Own Adventures

## Objective

After a review of the Ideas and Content Trait and a read-aloud experience, the student will use qualities of this trait when writing about his or her own make-believe adventure(s).

## Standards

- Standard 1J: Writes in a variety of formats (e.g., picture books, letters, stories, poems, information pieces)

## Materials

- copy of *Little Bear* by Else Holmelund Minarik
- puppet patterns (page 11), one or two per student
- craft sticks
- crayons or markers

## Lesson Opening

Ask students, "Have you ever gone on an imaginary adventure? Where did you go? What did you do?"

## Lesson Directions

1. Read *Little Bear* aloud to the class. (See Bibliography on page 92.)

2. Discuss with students how the author incorporated qualities of the Ideas and Content Trait in her writing. For example, Else Minarik connects her writing to her own experience, uses specific details, shows rather than tells, and develops the story.

3. Demonstrate the fact that every element of writing should add something to the whole. Do this by selecting sentences or passages of the book and asking students what would happen if the sentences or passages were removed.

4. Have students think of an imaginary adventure they would like to have. If the class needs a prompt, display the following story starter: "I have _____ and I am going to. . . ."

5. After they have written, have the students illustrate their stories by making puppets. Distribute copies of page 11 or have students design their own puppets based on characters in their story.

6. Have students share their completed stories with a partner, telling the story using their puppets.

## Lesson Closing

"You've heard stories from one or more of your classmates. How can the qualities of the Ideas and Content trait help you when writing stories? What happens if the author does not follow these guidelines (he or she does not include specific details or does not write clearly)?"

## Extension Activity

Discuss the following questions: "Do you have any relatives who say or do unique things? How do you react to them? Think of a time in your family when something unusual happened just because one person acted in a certain way." Have students write about a specific event that has occurred in their families. Use the following prompt if needed: When [a relative] came to visit, [an event that happened].

# Puppet Patterns

# Bear Ideas

## Objective

Given a coloring activity, the student will generate ideas and use the writing process to write a story.

## Standards

- Standard 1A: Prewriting: uses prewriting strategies to plan written work (e.g., draws pictures to generate ideas, writes key thoughts and questions)
- Standard 1B: Uses graphic organizers, story maps, and webs; groups related ideas; takes notes; brainstorms ideas
- Standard 1D: Elaborates on a central idea, uses paragraphs to develop separate ideas

## Materials

- coloring page (page 13), one copy per student
- colored pencils and/or crayons

## Lesson Opening

Introduce the concept of the writing process. List (or otherwise graphically display on the board) the following:

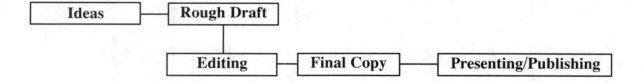

## Lesson Directions

1. Review the characteristics of the Ideas and Content Trait.
2. Distribute the coloring page. Tell students to think about a specific animal depicted on the page, or animals in general, as they color. Every time they think of an idea, word, phrase, etc., for their writing, they are to turn their paper over and write down the idea.
3. Allow students to work for 10–15 minutes.
4. Ask for volunteers to share their ideas. Collect papers for use at a later time.

## Lesson Closing

Ask students if they feel ready to write using their ideas. If time allows, have students begin work on a rough draft.

# Bear Ideas *(cont.)*

# Tools for a Successful Hunt

**Objective**

Given a graphic organizer, the student will write his or her ideas to use in developing content in writing.

**Standards**

- Standard 1A: Uses prewriting strategies to plan written work (e.g., discusses ideas with peers, draws pictures to generate ideas, writes key thoughts and questions, rehearses ideas, records reactions and observations)

- Standard 1D: Elaborates on a central idea, uses paragraphs to develop separate ideas

- Standard 1J: Writes in a variety of formats (e.g., picture books, letters, stories, poems, information pieces)

**Materials**

- "My Ideas" (page 15), one per student

- "Food for Thought" (page 16), overhead transparency and one copy per student

**Lesson Opening**

Ask students how a bear learns to survive in an often hostile environment (e.g., learns from mother, investigates, explores, uses sense of smell). In the same way, investigating and exploring ideas help a writer to develop the content of his or her writing.

**Lesson Directions**

1. Distribute "My Ideas" (page 15) and review the concept of brainstorming. Direct students' attention to the bear poster titled "Where Do Ideas Come From?" Ask students to brainstorm for a set time period (e.g., two minutes). Students will list specific ideas that they personally could write about.

2. Review characteristics of the Ideas and Content Trait, using the bear poster.

3. Distribute "Food for Thought" (page 16). You may need to discuss the graphic organizer one step at a time, beginning with topic, explaining each area to the class. Model on the board or overhead, if necessary.

4. Have students choose one topic from "My Ideas" to expand in detail. Students will fill in areas of page 15 with relevant details, experiences, knowledge, and examples.

5. Give students 10–15 minutes to write a paragraph or two expanding on their idea, experience, or example from "Food for Thought."

**Lesson Closing**

Say to students, "Now you have some ideas and information with which to begin to write. What ideas excite you enough to write about?" Tell students to keep these pages in their writing folders, as they may use them another day.

# My Ideas

**Directions:** Use this page to brainstorm topics of interest to you. The pictures on the page can help you get started.

# Food for Thought

**Directions:** Use this page to organize your ideas about one of your topics from page 15.

**Details**

_____

_____

_____

_____

**Examples**

_____

_____

_____

**Topic**

_____

_____

_____

_____

**Experiences**

_____

_____

_____

_____

**What You Know**

_____

_____

_____

_____

# Examine the Evidence

**Objective**

Given verbal prompts, the student will construct a story map of his or her life to date.

**Standards**

- Standard 1A:  Uses prewriting strategies to plan written work (e.g., discusses ideas with peers, draws pictures to generate ideas, writes key thoughts and questions, rehearses ideas, records reactions and observations)

- Standard 1G:  Dictates or writes detailed descriptions of familiar persons, places, objects, or experiences

- Standard 4B:  Uses a variety of strategies to identify topics to investigate (e.g., brainstorms, lists questions, uses idea webs)

**Materials**

- large sheets of drawing paper
- colored pencils

**Lesson Opening**

Ask students to remember the first day's discussion about bears.  Say, "The mother teaches her cubs what they need to know.  They survive by using what they have already learned."

**Lesson Directions**

1. Have students draw a line—straight, curved, etc.—to represent their life to date.

2. Go through landmarks for the map one at a time, having students use a different colored pencil for each one.  Consider asking students to draw a picture for each event.  You may need to explain each concept as you present it.  Model on the board with your own life story map.

   - main events (birth, start of school, etc.)—**brown**
   - good times, special events (birthdays, other special holidays, vacations, etc.)—**red**
   - one or two times when something sad happened—**blue**
   - when special people came into your life (friends, teachers, coaches)—**green**
   - things you have learned (riding a bike)—**purple**

3. Choose an event—from your own story map or a student's—and do a sample writing exercise to illustrate constructing a story from what you know.

4. Ask students to select one experience from their story maps about which they could write.

5. Explain "free writing" rules:  keep writing, stay silent, don't stop to correct spelling.  Direct students to write a paragraph or short story about the event they have chosen from their story map.  Give them 10–15 minutes of free writing time, then allow them to continue on their own as long as students need and/or interest dictates.

6. Collect and save the story maps for use with "The Many Voices of…" (page 47).

**Lesson Closing**

Call on two or three students to surprise the class with what they know.  Ask how they could build upon this experience to write a story.

# Using the Bear Senses

## Objective

Given things to see, touch, hear, smell, and taste, the student will write his or her observations using clear writing in such a way as to show, rather than tell, the reader of his or her experience.

## Standards

- Standard 1G: Dictates or writes detailed descriptions of familiar persons, places, objects, or experiences
- Standard 1J: Writes in a variety of formats (e.g., picture books, letters, stories, poems, information pieces)

## Materials

- objects to look at, touch, and smell (pictures of Arctic; ice cubes; dried fish; etc.) for three centers
- cassette or CD of instrumental music for listening center (e.g., nature sounds)
- small snack (e.g., frozen blueberries, bits of dried fish) placed into paper cups for taste center

## Preparation

Set up the centers, one for each of the five senses. Be sure to check for food allergies or to get parent permission before passing out any food.

## Lesson Opening

Tell students that while bears have an excellent sense of smell, they cannot hear or see very well. Remind them that bears survive by exploring and observing the world around them. Say, "Today you will have the opportunity to use all of your senses to experience a bear's world."

## Lesson Directions

1. Review characteristics of the trait. Ask students what is meant by "show, don't tell."
2. Ask students to name the five senses and what they do. (They give us information about the world around us.) Ask students how using our senses can help in writing. (The use of sensory information helps writers to focus on a topic and use specific details.)
3. Divide the class into five groups, and send one group to each center to experience using one of their senses.
4. When the students have experienced each center, have them do one of the following exercises:
   - Write about their favorite sensory experience and why this is so.
   - Write one sentence about each sensory experience.

## Lesson Closing

Review the process of gathering data and generating ideas. Remind students that just as a bear uses its instincts and previously learned knowledge to reach a successful conclusion to the hunt, writers must communicate their ideas in a clearly written piece of work.

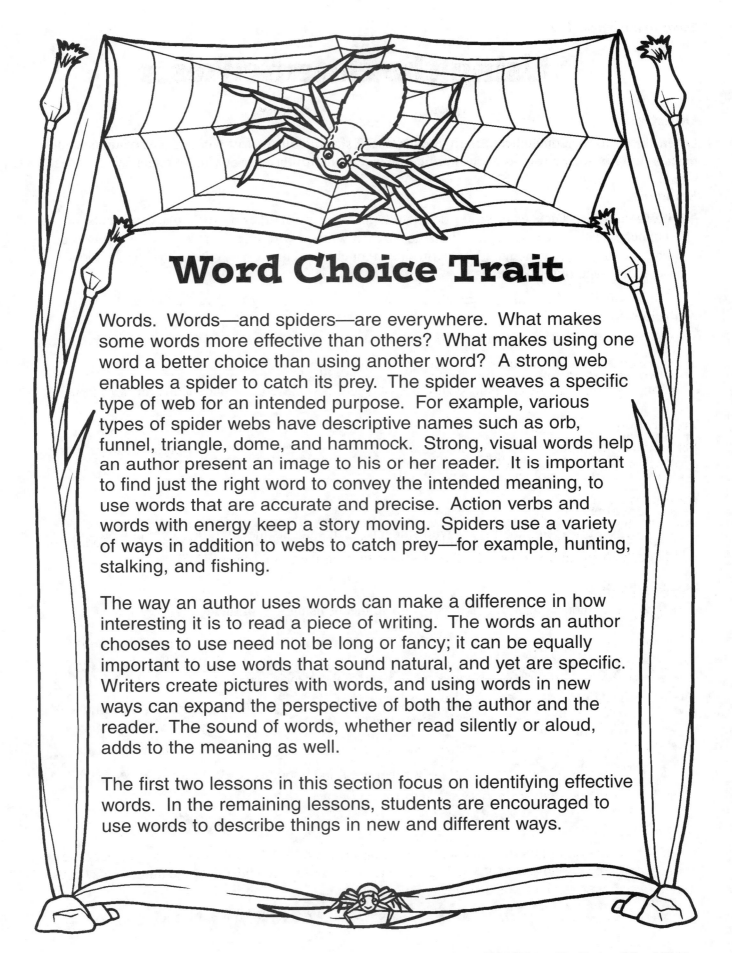

# Word Choice Trait

Words. Words—and spiders—are everywhere. What makes some words more effective than others? What makes using one word a better choice than using another word? A strong web enables a spider to catch its prey. The spider weaves a specific type of web for an intended purpose. For example, various types of spider webs have descriptive names such as orb, funnel, triangle, dome, and hammock. Strong, visual words help an author present an image to his or her reader. It is important to find just the right word to convey the intended meaning, to use words that are accurate and precise. Action verbs and words with energy keep a story moving. Spiders use a variety of ways in addition to webs to catch prey—for example, hunting, stalking, and fishing.

The way an author uses words can make a difference in how interesting it is to read a piece of writing. The words an author chooses to use need not be long or fancy; it can be equally important to use words that sound natural, and yet are specific. Writers create pictures with words, and using words in new ways can expand the perspective of both the author and the reader. The sound of words, whether read silently or aloud, adds to the meaning as well.

The first two lessons in this section focus on identifying effective words. In the remaining lessons, students are encouraged to use words to describe things in new and different ways.

# Catching Excellent Words

## Objective

Given the basic characteristics of the Word Choice Trait, the student will compile lists of words that make writing more interesting, as well as words that do not fit the trait of word choice, and put these words in the appropriate places on a poster(s).

## Standards

- Standard 1A: Uses prewriting strategies to plan written work (e.g., discusses ideas with peers, draws pictures to generate ideas, writes key thoughts and questions, rehearses ideas, records reactions and observations)

- Standard 1B: Uses graphic organizers, story maps, and webs; groups related ideas; takes notes; brainstorms ideas

## Materials

- two large sheets of poster board
- black string (optional)

## Preparation

Decorate each sheet of poster board to look like a different type of spider web. Label one poster "Pesky Words" and the other "Attractive Words."

## Lesson Opening

Briefly discuss spiders and their webs with students. Tell students they will be catching words that are "pests" in a web.

## Lesson Directions

1. Teach the students that effective word choice means using the following:

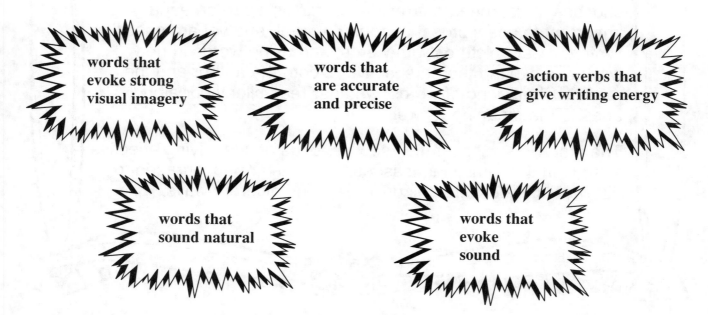

words that evoke strong visual imagery

words that are accurate and precise

action verbs that give writing energy

words that sound natural

words that evoke sound

# Catching Excellent Words *(cont.)*

**Lesson Directions** *(cont.)*

2.  Ask students what types of words would be interesting to read. Explain that "effective" word choice means using words that help the reader understand what the author is writing. Discuss how some words are too general or overused in student writing. Give examples. Ask students to volunteer some "pesky" words. Write the words on the first spider web poster.

3.  Brainstorm words that fit the positive qualities of this trait. Ask students to think of words that will catch the attention of the reader and make him or her want to read the writing. Record these words on the second spider web poster, using the sample words listed below as prompts if necessary. Explain that "attractive" in this context means words that attract the reader to the writing.

**Sample Words**

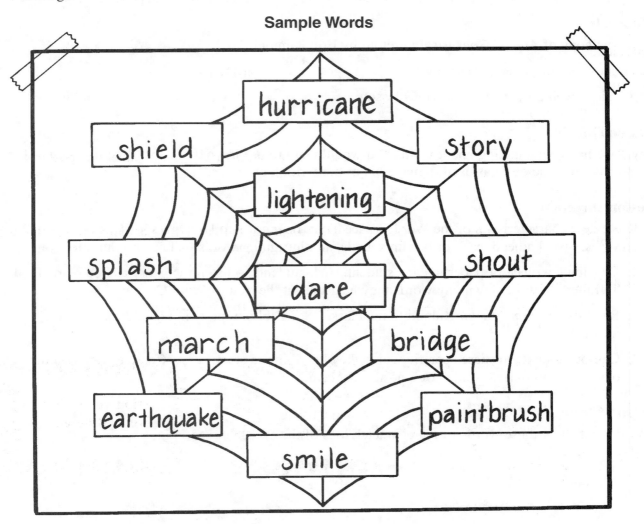

**Lesson Closing**

Review qualities of the Word Choice Trait, if necessary. Tell the class you will be saving the posters to refer to on subsequent days.

# Spinning a Web

**Objective**

Given a selection from literature, the student will become aware of how an author uses word choice by identifying words that do or do not meet the criteria of the Word Choice Trait.

**Standards**

- Standard 1F:  Evaluates own and others' writing (e.g., asks questions and makes comments about writing)
- Standard 1I:  Writes in response to literature
- Standard 1J:  Writes in a variety of formats

**Materials**

- one copy of *Anansi Goes Fishing* retold by Eric Kimmel
- one piece of paper per student
- spider-web posters from previous lesson

**Lesson Opening**

Say, "We have been talking about words you would want to use in your writing.  Today you will listen for words someone else has used to make his or her writing effective."

**Lesson Directions**

1. Review characteristics of the Word Choice Trait, listing the following:  specific nouns, action verbs, visual adjectives, words with sounds, and intriguing words that catch your attention.

2. Distribute a piece of paper to each student.  Ask students to listen to a story as you read aloud. Tell them to write down any words they hear that fit the trait of Word Choice.

3. Read *Anansi Goes Fishing* aloud to the class.  (See Bibliography on page 92 for book information.)

4. Call on students to share specific words they heard in the story.  List effective words on the board or on the appropriate spider-web poster displayed.

**Lesson Closing**

Ask students how these words fit the characteristics of the Word Choice Trait.

# Poetic Words

## Objective

Given index cards and a class-generated list of words, the student will label classroom objects in a novel way to expand his or her perspective.

## Standards

- **Standard 1A:** Uses prewriting strategies to plan written work (e.g., discusses ideas with peers, draws pictures to generate ideas, writes key thoughts and questions, rehearses ideas, records reactions and observations)

- **Standard 2B:** Uses descriptive language that clarifies and enhances ideas (e.g., describes familiar people, places, or objects)

## Materials

- index cards, three per student

- one copy of *poemcrazy* by Susan G. Wooldridge (optional, for teacher reference)

## Lesson Opening

Ask students, "What are some of your favorite words? Why? What do you like about these words?"

## Lesson Directions

1. Write some student-volunteered favorite words on the board.

2. Read some word samples from *poemcrazy* (pages 12, 13, 16, and 18). (See Bibliography on page 92 for book information.)

3. Introduce the concept of "word tickets" (*poemcrazy*, pages 14–18). Explain to students that they will write words on index cards (one word per card, three cards per student). Do not tell students their next task until they have written their words.

4. Have students use the cards to label objects around the room. Cards may be propped up next to the object or taped to it (e.g., to the door). Emphasize that the labels will not make sense! They may end up with a paintbrush window, a rainbow wall, thunder art, etc.

5. Once students have finished, you may walk around the room and read the labeled objects to them. Or, you may want students to discover labeled objects for themselves.

6. Ask students if the labels change the way they see these things. Explain further, if necessary, with an illustration of coloring outside the lines or stepping outside of the box.

7. Have students write a poem about something they saw differently.

## Lesson Closing

Ask student volunteers to read and share their poems with the class.

# Web Pictures

## Objective

Given many words from which to choose, students will create collages that express specific ideas.

## Standards

- Standard 1K: Writes expressive composition (e.g., expresses ideas, reflections, and observations; uses an individual, authentic voice; uses relevant details; and presents ideas that enable a reader to imagine the world of the event or experience)

## Materials

- old magazines that are language appropriate for classroom use and/or newspapers (you may wish to enlist volunteer help to pre-cut a variety of words and phrases for your students to use)
- 9" x 12" (23 cm x 30 cm) colored construction paper, one per student
- scissors (optional)
- glue

## Lesson Opening

Ask students if they have ever heard of a "word picture." Tell students they will create a picture with words instead of drawings.

## Lesson Directions

1. Review characteristics of the Word Choice Trait.

2. Explain and discuss the concept of a word collage. A word collage contains words that communicate thoughts and feelings to another person. Model a cluster of words on the board. Begin with a specific word (e.g., "sunset" or "spider web"). Ask students to volunteer words to paint a picture.

3. Encourage students to think of an idea or concept of their own (e.g., peace, rest, family, etc.) that they would like to express using words.

4. Distribute one piece of plain scratch paper to each student. Have them write one word at the top of the paper. Tell them this is what their word picture will describe.

5. Have students list words to describe or tell about their idea.

6. Tell the class they will create a word collage using letters and/or words from magazines.

7. Tell students they are not to use their original word in their collage. Challenge students to use effective words so others will be able to guess their idea.

8. Distribute one piece of construction paper to each student. Introduce the activity of cutting words from magazines (if not pre-cut) and gluing them on the paper to make a word collage.

9. If time permits, ask students to write a story based on their word collages. Students may share their collages and stories with the class.

## Lesson Closing

Select students at random to share their collages. Have the class first guess what idea they think is being portrayed in the collage. Next, have students read specific words and describe why these words were included. Ask students what makes these words effective. (Refer to the "Attractive Words" poster during discussion, if necessary.)

# Finding Your Way Through the Web

**Objective**

Given a review of descriptive words, the student will write a descriptive paragraph and draw a map or illustration.

**Standards**

- Standard 1B: Uses graphic organizers, story maps, and webs; groups related ideas; takes notes; brainstorms ideas

- Standard 1H: Dictates or writes detailed descriptions of familiar persons, places, objects, or experiences

- Standard 1J: Writes in a variety of formats (e.g., picture books, letters, stories, poems, information pieces)

- Standard 1K: Writes expressive composition (e.g., expresses ideas, reflections, and observations; uses an individual, authentic voice; uses relevant details; and presents ideas that enable a reader to imagine the world of the event or experience)

- Standard 2B: Uses descriptive language that clarifies and enhances ideas (e.g., describes familiar people, places, or objects)

**Materials**

- plain white construction paper

- colored pencils

- scratch paper

**Lesson Opening**

Have students think of their favorite place. Ask them to consider why this place is special.

**Lesson Directions**

1. Review characteristics of the Word Choice Trait. Discuss descriptive words in particular, giving examples if necessary.

2. Have students make a list of words on scratch paper describing their favorite place. Encourage them to use specific, visual words.

3. Direct the class to use those words to write a descriptive paragraph, using complete sentences. Tell them they may wish to include directions to their special place.

4. Students may then draw a map to the place or a picture to go with their descriptive paragraph.

**Lesson Closing**

Have students read their descriptive paragraph(s) aloud to the class without showing the illustrations. Ask the class if they could visualize the place based on the descriptive words the author used.

# Be an Engineer

## Objective
Given examples from advertising, the student will create a product and then write an advertisement for it.

## Standards
- Standard 1B: Uses graphic organizers, story maps, and webs; groups related ideas; takes notes; brainstorms ideas

- Standard 1J: Writes in a variety of formats (e.g., picture books, letters, stories, poems, information pieces)

## Materials
- sample advertisements and/or product descriptions
- "My New Invention" (page 27)

## Preparation
Reproduce page 27 onto an overhead transparency and reproduce one copy per student

## Lesson Opening
Say, "Earlier we read *Anansi Goes Fishing*, a folk tale describing how spiders may have learned to weave their webs. A new invention was created out of an activity Anansi enjoyed."

## Lesson Directions
1. Discuss the Word Choice Trait, particularly as it relates to writing product descriptions (e.g., precise word use, action verbs, high energy language, how words sound, etc.)
2. Display sample advertisements and descriptions on an overhead, chart, or board; or distribute them among students if there are enough samples. Discuss how the people who write the ads catch the reader's attention with the words and pictures they choose to use. Identify words meeting the criteria for the Word Choice Trait. Note their use, if applicable (e.g., action words).
3. Ask students to think of something they like to do. How could that activity create a new invention? Or, ask students "What if you were creating a new recipe, a new game, or a new toy?" Give examples, if necessary (e.g., making a board game for a relative for a Christmas gift, experimenting in the kitchen and developing a new cookie recipe, etc.).
4. Show the overhead of "My New Invention." Ask students what information a reader would need to know about their new product/invention. Brainstorm ideas and list them on the board.
5. Distribute page 27. Have students work individually or with a partner to invent a product. Students should fill in each box on the work sheet as it pertains to their product. Remind students to use specific and descriptive words that have qualities of strong word choice.
6. Select as many partners as time allows for reading their descriptions to the class. Ask students if they can tell what product is being described by the partners' advertisement. Would they want to buy this product? Why or why not?

## Lesson Closing
Have students identify specific words used that were effective. Add the words to the spider web word poster. As an option, have students bind advertisements into a class magazine.

# My New Invention

**Name of your invention**

| **What does your invention look like?** | **What does it do?** |
|---|---|

**How do you use it?**

| **How is the invention special or different from others?** | **Who might use it?** | **How will it benefit people?** |
|---|---|---|

**Is it for sale?  How can someone buy your invention?**

**Illustration of your invention**

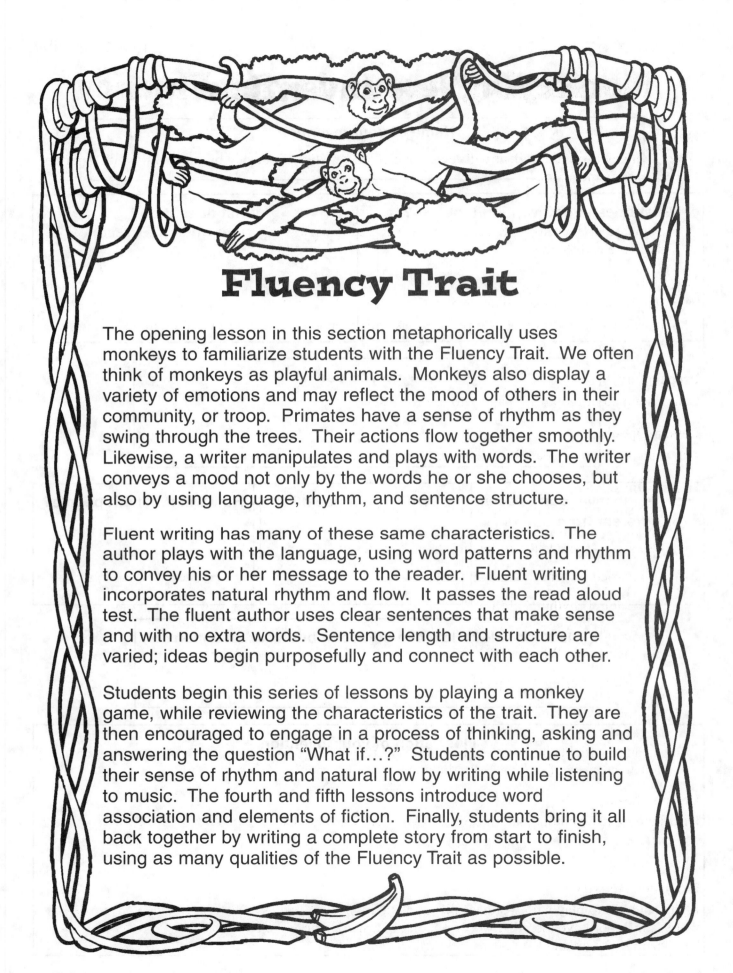

# Fluency Trait

The opening lesson in this section metaphorically uses monkeys to familiarize students with the Fluency Trait. We often think of monkeys as playful animals. Monkeys also display a variety of emotions and may reflect the mood of others in their community, or troop. Primates have a sense of rhythm as they swing through the trees. Their actions flow together smoothly. Likewise, a writer manipulates and plays with words. The writer conveys a mood not only by the words he or she chooses, but also by using language, rhythm, and sentence structure.

Fluent writing has many of these same characteristics. The author plays with the language, using word patterns and rhythm to convey his or her message to the reader. Fluent writing incorporates natural rhythm and flow. It passes the read aloud test. The fluent author uses clear sentences that make sense and with no extra words. Sentence length and structure are varied; ideas begin purposefully and connect with each other.

Students begin this series of lessons by playing a monkey game, while reviewing the characteristics of the trait. They are then encouraged to engage in a process of thinking, asking and answering the question "What if…?" Students continue to build their sense of rhythm and natural flow by writing while listening to music. The fourth and fifth lessons introduce word association and elements of fiction. Finally, students bring it all back together by writing a complete story from start to finish, using as many qualities of the Fluency Trait as possible.

# Monkeying Around with Fluency

**Objective**

Given monkey toys, the student will review the characteristics of fluency by interacting with a partner and other class members.

**Standards**

- Standard 2: Develops awareness of stylistic and rhetorical aspects of writing (i.e., sentence structure and rhythm)

**Materials**

- jungle pattern for classroom display (page 30)
- plastic monkey toys (e.g., Barrel of Monkeys™), enough for class to work in groups of four
- "Monkey Antics" (page 31)

**Preparation**

Enlarge and color the jungle pattern to use for display.

**Lesson Opening**

Ask students what is meant by fluency in writing. Use fluent reading as an example.

**Lesson Directions**

1. Ask students what they know about monkeys. List monkey characteristics on board or overhead.

2. Teach the trait by comparing monkey behavior to fluent writing. Give examples as you go, if necessary. Include the following characteristics of fluent writing:

   - varied sentence length and structure

   - natural rhythm and flow

   - uses a process of thinking (e.g., asks the question, "What if…?")

   - uses differing word patterns

   - plays with language

   - has clear sentences that make sense

   - has ideas that begin purposefully and connect to one another

   - matches the mood

   - has no extra words

   - passes the read-aloud test

3. Arrange students in groups of four. Have students play the monkey game, reviewing and naming a characteristic of the trait each time they pick up a monkey.

**Lesson Closing**

Distribute monkey cutout patterns, one or two to each group. Have students program each cutout with one characteristic of the trait. Display the monkeys on the jungle poster.

**Extension Activity**

Invite students to play with words as they pick up monkeys. For example, have students name rhyming word families or have them list words relating to a specific topic (e.g., swinging). You may wish to have them make up and list nonsense words as well.

# Jungle Pattern

**Directions:** Enlarge as necessary for classroom display.

# Monkey Antics

# What If...?

## Objective

Given a read-aloud experience with literature, the student will experiment with word patterns and language by writing his or her own story.

## Standards

- Standard 1F: Evaluates own and others' writing (e.g., asks questions and makes comments about writing, helps classmates apply grammatical and mechanical conventions)
- Standard 1I: Writes in response to literature
- Standard 2A: Uses general, frequently used words to convey basic ideas
- Standard 2C: Uses a variety of sentence structures

## Materials

- one copy of *Curious George Gets a Job* (Note: any Curious George book may be used.)
- jungle pattern on display in classroom
- "What If...?" (page 33), one copy per student

## Lesson Opening

Ask students how writing might have natural rhythm and flow. Review the comparison between monkeys and fluency.

## Lesson Directions

1. Draw students' attention to the fluency poster displayed. Go over characteristics of fluency with students, stressing natural rhythm (achieved by varied sentence length), ideas that begin purposefully and connect to one another, a process of thinking (asking "What if?"), word patterns, and play with language.

2. Ask students to listen for these specific elements of fluency as you read the story *Curious George Gets a Job* aloud to the class.

3. Distribute page 33 and introduce the "What If...?" ideas for stories and/or poetry. Have students write for a given amount of time, 10–15 minutes. Encourage them to focus on the qualities listed on the fluency poster as they write.

4. Ask for volunteers to share their stories with the class.

## Lesson Closing

Ask students to think about the Curious George story (stories). What elements of fluency did they hear? In what ways did the author use rhythm, a variety of sentence structures, word patterns, or play with language to tell a story?

# What If...? *(cont.)*

### Story Ideas for *Curious George Gets a Job*

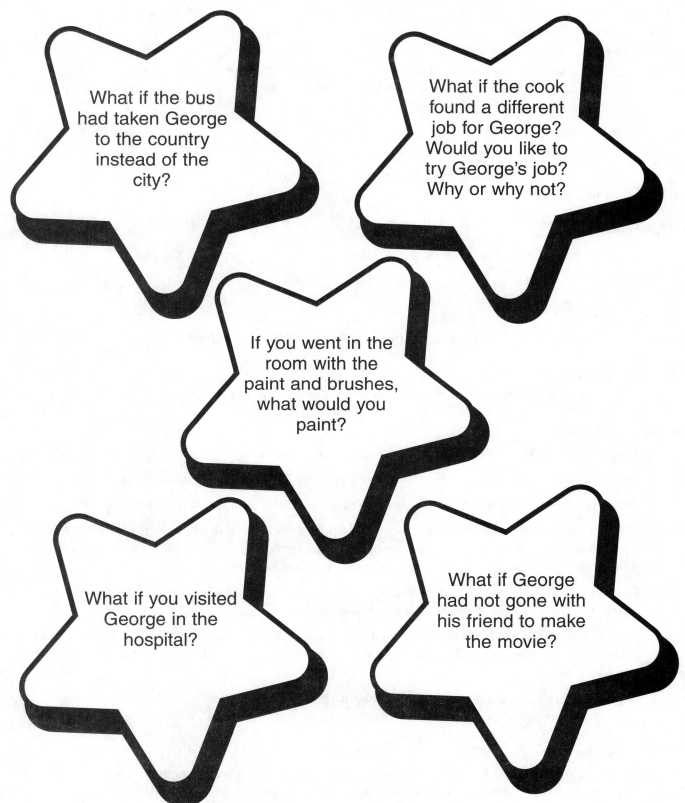

What if the bus had taken George to the country instead of the city?

What if the cook found a different job for George? Would you like to try George's job? Why or why not?

If you went in the room with the paint and brushes, what would you paint?

What if you visited George in the hospital?

What if George had not gone with his friend to make the movie?

# Climbing a Tree

## Objective

Given one or more word prompts, the student will design a web using word association.

## Standards

- Standard 1A: Uses prewriting strategies to plan written work (e.g., discusses ideas with peers, draws pictures to generate ideas, writes key thoughts and questions, rehearses ideas, records reactions and observations)

- Standard 1B: Uses graphic organizers, story maps, and webs; groups related ideas; takes notes; brainstorms ideas

- Standard 1J: Writes in a variety of formats (e.g., picture books, letters, stories, poems, information pieces)

## Materials

- "Climbing a Tree" (page 35), one per student
- colored pencils (optional)
- blank white paper

## Preparation

Enlarge "Climbing a Tree" (page 35), or copy it onto an overhead transparency.

## Lesson Opening

Ask students how and where monkeys often play (e.g., climbing in and hanging from trees).

## Lesson Directions

1. Display "Climbing a Tree" (page 35) on the overhead or on the board.

2. Review the Fluency Trait, emphasizing that ideas begin purposefully and connect to one another.

3. Ask 6 or 7 students to volunteer a word. Write the words on or around the tree outline.

4. Explain the concept of word association. Select one word from those written. Model writing a word or words that you think of when you hear that particular word. Ask for volunteers to give words, one at a time, as you continue to model word association.

5. Distribute copies of page 35. Have students think of a word, or allow them to use one of the words from the class discussion as a starting point.

6. Tell students to write down the first word they think of when they hear their starting word. Have them continue to write words, one at a time, around the branches of their tree to create a word cluster or web.

7. Have students choose a group of words and/or related ideas, to write about. Students may write a short story, poem, or 1–2 informative paragraphs, at your discretion.

## Lesson Closing

Ask students if their writing had a logical progression of ideas, with one thought connecting to the next. Ask if this makes their writing flow more smoothly. Why might this be so?

# Climbing a Tree *(cont.)*

## Graphic Organizer

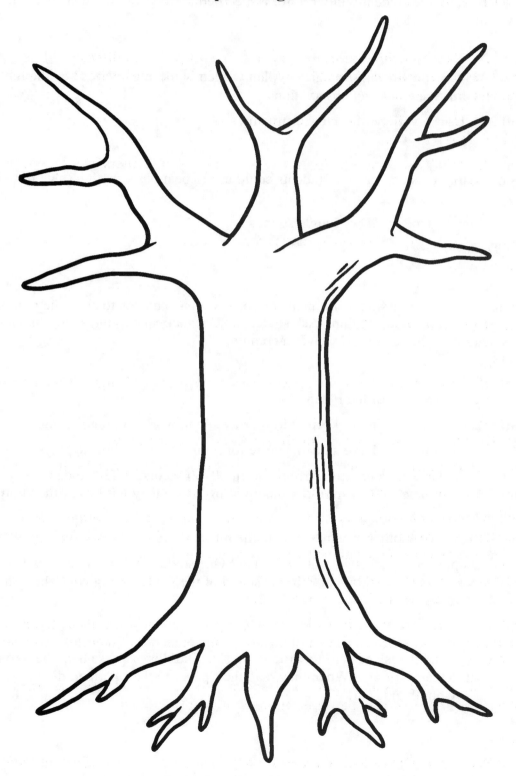

# Jungle Music

## Objective

Given music to listen to, the student will write for a specified period of time, then check his or her writing for rhythms.

## Standards

- Standard 1A: Uses prewriting strategies to plan written work (e.g., writes key thoughts and questions, records reactions and observations)
- Standard 2C: Uses a variety of sentence structures

## Materials

- percussion instruments and objects students could use to beat out a rhythm (e.g., dowels or spoons)
- instrumental music tape or CD of jungle sounds
- tape or CD player

## Lesson Opening

Beat out a rhythm on the percussion instruments or objects. Ask students to copy the rhythm with their hands on their desks. Talk about rhythm. Ask students, "Does human talking sound like music? Why or why not? What do talking and music have in common?"

## Lesson Directions

1. Review the characteristics of the Fluency Trait.
2. Review the rules of free writing: keep writing, stay silent, work without editing.
3. Play the instrumental tape. Have students write for 5 minutes while music plays.
4. When time is up, have students stop writing. Wait 30–60 seconds. Tell students they will write again for 5 more minutes. They may continue writing where they left off, or they may begin with a new thought.
5. Time the students for another 5 minutes while the music plays.
6. When time is up, have students get with a partner. One student will read his or her paper, and the partner will beat out any rhythm that is in the sound of the words, using his or her hands lightly on the desk. Switch roles.

## Lesson Closing

Ask students if they found it easy or hard to write to music. Did this exercise help them to put "natural rhythm and flow" into their writing? When they read their paper to their partner, did the writing have more of a sense of rhythm than usual?

# It's a _____ Day in the Jungle

## Objective

Given an introduction to story elements, the student will create a story in written and pictorial form.

## Standards

- Standard 1A: Uses prewriting strategies to plan written work (e.g., uses graphic organizers, groups related ideas, takes notes, brainstorms ideas)

- Standard 1E: Uses strategies to edit and publish written work (e.g., proofreads using a dictionary and other resources; edits for grammar, punctuation, capitalization, and spelling at a developmentally appropriate level; incorporates illustrations or photos, shares finished product)

- Standard 2B: Uses descriptive language that clarifies and enhances ideas (e.g., describes familiar people, places, or objects)

## Materials

- five sheets of tagboard

- magazine pictures or other photos of monkeys and jungle scenes (optional)

- 4" x 6" (10 cm x 15 cm) index cards, five per student

- jungle poster for fluency on classroom display

## Preparation

Label the tagboard sheets as follows: "Character," "Setting of Place," "Setting of Time," "Mood," and "Action or Conflict." Find magazine pictures or other photos of monkeys and/or jungle scenes to make a visual display illustrating the heading on each card. Use these posters to designate stations around the classroom.

## Lesson Opening

Tell students monkeys display many different emotions and moods. Ask students to describe possible moods that might be found in a jungle story.

## Lesson Directions

1. Review characteristics of the Fluency Trait. Emphasize mood, word patterns, and the use of clear sentences that make sense.

2. One at a time, introduce fiction elements: character, setting (place), setting (time), mood, and conflict. These terms may be new to the students. Ask the class what every story needs. Define "conflict" as interesting action, or a problem to solve. Give examples of story ideas with and without conflict.

3. Have the class brainstorm specific examples for each element (e.g., characters: monkeys, gorillas; mood: angry, playful).

# It's a _____ Day in the Jungle *(cont.)*

**Lesson Directions** *(cont.)*

4. Divide the class into five groups and distribute five index cards to each student. Ask students to label the cards as follows: "Characters," "Setting of Place," "Setting of Time," "Mood," and "Conflict." Direct students to rotate through the stations designated by the posters, using the posters as springboards for ideas that they are to write on the appropriate index card. Allow students 2–3 minutes at each station.

5. After each group has visited all five stations, have students return to their seats and write a short story using the notes on their index cards. Their story will be titled, "It's a _____ Day in the Jungle."

6. Have students illustrate their stories, if time permits. Post the stories in a display titled, "It's a _____ Day in the Jungle."

**Lesson Closing**

Allow students to read the display. Ask them if they could determine the setting and mood of each of their classmate's writing. Ask the class how and why their writing is more fluent. (Student writing should begin to exhibit connection of ideas, natural rhythm, and clear sentences that make sense.)

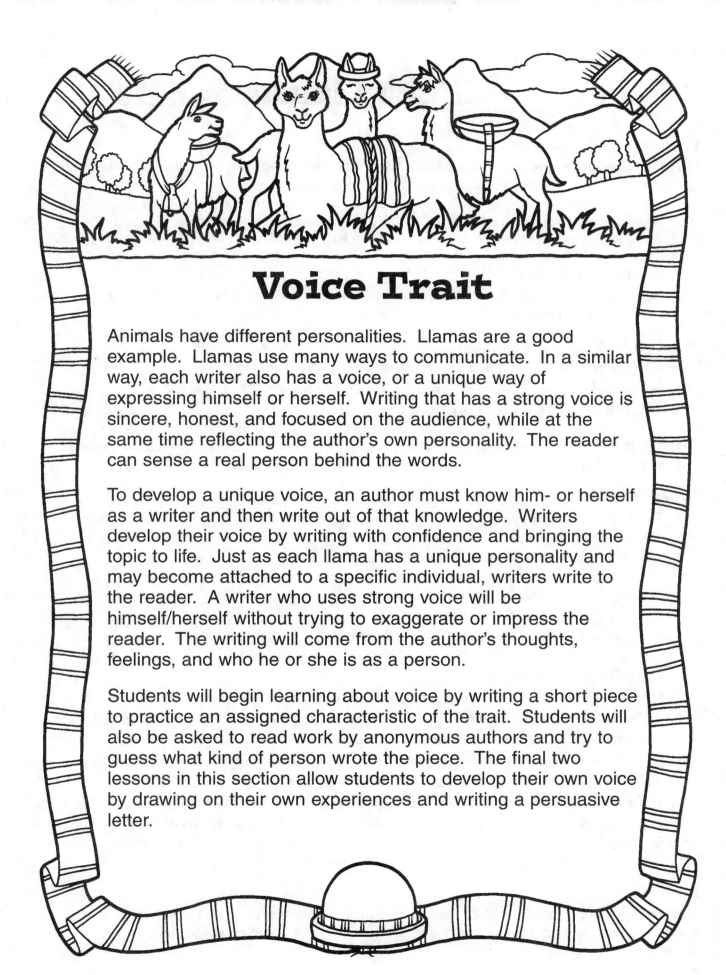

# Voice Trait

Animals have different personalities. Llamas are a good example. Llamas use many ways to communicate. In a similar way, each writer also has a voice, or a unique way of expressing himself or herself. Writing that has a strong voice is sincere, honest, and focused on the audience, while at the same time reflecting the author's own personality. The reader can sense a real person behind the words.

To develop a unique voice, an author must know him- or herself as a writer and then write out of that knowledge. Writers develop their voice by writing with confidence and bringing the topic to life. Just as each llama has a unique personality and may become attached to a specific individual, writers write to the reader. A writer who uses strong voice will be himself/herself without trying to exaggerate or impress the reader. The writing will come from the author's thoughts, feelings, and who he or she is as a person.

Students will begin learning about voice by writing a short piece to practice an assigned characteristic of the trait. Students will also be asked to read work by anonymous authors and try to guess what kind of person wrote the piece. The final two lessons in this section allow students to develop their own voice by drawing on their own experiences and writing a persuasive letter.

# I'm a Llama

## Objective

Given the characteristics of the trait, the student will practice writing using one particular quality of voice.

## Standards

- Standard 1A:  Uses prewriting strategies to plan written work (e.g., discusses ideas with peers, draws pictures to generate ideas, writes key thoughts and questions, rehearses ideas, records reactions and observations)
- Standard 1F:  Evaluates own and others' writing (e.g., asks questions and makes comments about writing, helps classmates apply grammatical and mechanical conventions)

## Materials

- llama pattern for classroom display (page 41)
- current news or magazine article about llamas (article on page 42 may be used)
- 3" x 5" index cards, several per student

## Lesson Opening

Ask students what they know about llamas.  Read the current news article aloud to the class.

## Lesson Directions

1. Teach the characteristics of the Voice Trait, using examples from the news article or other resource material about llamas.  Share with the students that voice does the following:
   - makes a piece sound a like a particular person wrote it
   - allows the author's personality to come through the writing
   - has natural rhythm
   - hooks the reader, calling attention to the writing
   - conveys honesty and requires self-knowledge
   - brings the topic to life
   - talks directly to the reader.
2. Compare characteristics of llamas to the qualities of the Voice Trait.
3. Tell students you will give them a word about which to write (e.g., llama, camel, desert).
4. Assign one characteristic of the trait to each student.
5. Have them write about the word(s) given, focusing on the assigned quality of the trait (e.g., a student assigned "brings the topic to life" will practice doing so as he or she writes about a llama).
6. When students have completed writing, select students to read their writing to the class.
7. Distribute index cards to the class.  Direct students to listen for specific qualities of the Voice Trait (as assigned) as their classmates read aloud.  Tell students they will write positive comments pertaining to the pieces they listen to, evaluating the use of voice.

## Lesson Closing

After each student reads, have other students give their comment slips to the reader.  Encourage students to read the comments at a later time and to show respect and good listening skills for fellow classmates.

# Llama Pattern

# Llamas

A camel without a hump? A good-natured relative of the camel, llamas are often used as pack animals. Their calm nature makes them easy to work with and train. Llamas don't complain, and they make good companions on long hikes. Sure-footed on rocks and slopes, their soft foot pads do not damage trails.

Llamas are social, herd animals. With training, they can become friendly and affectionate. They are curious and intelligent, and they have many ways of communicating. A llama may hum softly to express contentment. When upset or frightened, a llama makes short, high bleats or a high-pitched bray. Llamas use a shrill whine to signal alarm. A low hum shows anger, and an angry animal may spit. Llamas also position their ears to communicate alertness, listening, relaxation, or annoyance.

Llamas have long ears and a long neck. They have a small head with large eyes and a thin face. They stand 40"–45" (102–114 cm) tall at the shoulders and may weigh as much as 300–450 pounds (136–205 kg). A llama's thick wool is a valuable feature.

Llamas have played an important role in various civilizations for thousands of years. Today, these gentle animals are increasingly kept as pets. As people continue to rediscover their value, llamas are sure to become more popular.

# A Llama Says...

## Objective

After a read-aloud experience, the student will write pieces of dialogue as they might be spoken by different characters.

## Standards

- Standard 1I: Writes in response to literature

## Materials

- one copy of *My Mama Is a Llama* by Deborah Guarne
- "A Llama Says..." (page 44)

## Preparation

Reproduce one copy of page 44 for each student.

## Lesson Opening

Ask students, "Have you ever read stories where it seems like the characters are real? What makes it seem that way?"

## Lesson Directions

1. Guide students in reviewing characteristics of voice as the class discusses any books in which it seems the author is speaking directly to the reader. Also discuss realistic characters as portrayed in classroom books.

2. Read the book *My Mama Is a Llama* aloud to the class. (See Bibliography on page 92 for book information.) Discuss how the author's and characters' voices come through in the writing.

3. Distribute page 44. Using one of the characters from the story, model completing a conversation balloon for that character. Include the following questions: What might the character say? What words would the character use? What other characters might have been included in the story?

4. Have the class create an additional three characters of their own. They will then write the characters' words in a conversation bubble. Students should draw a picture of the character in the space provided and label the character on the line below.

5. Select students to read the characters' words from their papers and allow their classmates to try to guess what type of animal is speaking.

## Lesson Closing

Say to students, "In the story we read today, did it sound like the characters were real? Why or why not? Did the author say anything that made it feel like he or she was talking to you, the reader, directly? If so, what? What are some ways you could begin to use the qualities of this trait in your own writing?"

## Extension

Have students create rhyming riddles using characters they create.

# A Llama Says... *(cont.)*

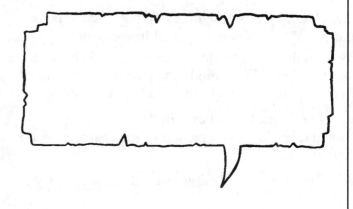

_____

_____

_____

_____

# Guess Who Is Talking

## Objective

Given writing samples, the student will become familiar with voice by answering specific questions. Given a description of a fictional character, the student will write in the "person's" voice.

## Standards

- Standard 1F: Evaluates own and others' writing (e.g., asks questions and makes comments about writing, helps classmates apply grammatical and mechanical conventions)
- Standard 1J: Writes in a variety of formats (e.g., picture books, letters, stories, poems, information pieces)

## Materials

- "Guess Who Is Talking" (pages 46)

## Preparation

Copy page 46 onto either one transparency or onto five separate transparencies so that you can display the writing samples one at a time to students.

## Lesson Opening

Ask students if they read a story without the author's name on it if they could identify who wrote it. What clues might they use to identify the author?

## Lesson Directions

1. Review the characteristics of the Voice Trait.

2. Show one overhead or one sample at a time from pages 46. Ask the students questions about each piece of writing:

   - Who do you think wrote this?
   - Who is talking? Is it a male or female? How old is the person?
   - What might this person's job or favorite activities be?
   - Does the writing sound like a real person talking?

3. List specific character(s) on the board—for example, a 15-year-old soccer player, a 50-year-old book seller, a college student, etc. Have students write a letter to the class in the voice of one character.

## Lesson Closing

Read two or three student paragraphs aloud without identifying the authors. Ask the class if they can match the paragraph to a character on the board, and if so, which one. Does it sound like that "person" wrote it? Or did the student's own voice come through? How could they tell?

# Guess Who Is Talking *(cont.)*

**Sample Paragraph #1**

I feel like I am in the North Pole. I met a couple of friends on my way. I met a polar bear, monkey, and a wolf, too. I stopped for a rest and then I said, "Hey! How are you? I am Nick. Oh! I remember you. I saw you at the farm." So he paddled to the iceberg and they caught lots of fish.

**Sample Paragraph #2**

I love penguins. He plays with his best best friends. A penguin got lost. Oh dear, I need to find him. They searched all over but they can't find him. They almost gave up. He was in a cave. I miss my mommy and daddy. They almost found him. They got up and looked very very hard. They looked in the wrong cave. Oops, I stepped on your toe. Now they went and they found him.

**Sample Paragraph #3**

If I were someone who had the choice to choose a power that influenced the earth, the power I would choose would be control of the weather. I would choose this because it would mean a sunny summer. . . . It would mean a snowy winter for those who like snow. I could even ride clouds. I could make a decent snow fort! My friends and I could have a good snowball fight.

**Sample Paragraph #4**

I am happy to report that our 650-mile trip from Haines to Fairbanks was made without difficulty under ideal weather conditions for this time of year. Our VW Rabbit performed beautifully in spite of near 40 below zero weather in one spot along the way.

**Sample Paragraph #5**

Resting and recuperating?

Uh, well, I did slip out from work for a Friday and a Monday in San Clemente with my family. The "vacation" was tiny, yes, but it helped me recharge.

I know I need to do a better job on that count, but change takes time.

**Sample Paragraph #6**

Silently, I walked up to the edge of the crowd. They were all intent, watching some activity out in the middle of the courtyard. I stood on my toes and tried to see over the heads of those standing in front of me. Every now and then I could catch a glimpse of bright color, in a sudden flash of movement.

# The Many Voices of...

## Objective

Given prompts, the student will consider aspects of his or her life that can provide material for his or her writing by adding to previously begun story maps.

## Standards

- Standard 1A: Uses prewriting strategies to plan written work (e.g., discusses ideas with peers, draws pictures to generate ideas, writes key thoughts and questions, rehearses ideas, records reactions and observations)
- Standard 1L: Writes autobiographical compositions (e.g., provides a context within which the incident occurs, uses simple narrative strategies, provides some insight into why this incident is memorable)

## Materials

- student story maps (see page 17)
- colored pencils
- llama pattern on classroom display

## Lesson Opening

Remind students of the story maps they created earlier. Tell them they will be adding to that page today, and that they will also practice writing in their voice.

## Lesson Directions

1. Ask students to put their heads down and listen quietly while you ask them some questions. Tell them not to raise their hands but to think of their answers silently.
2. Ask students, "Who are you? When do you feel the most like you?" Students may need to be reminded not to look at each other or laugh.
3. Distribute story maps to students, if they don't have them readily available in their writing folders.
4. Review and discuss characteristics of the Voice Trait, using the class poster or other visual aids.
5. Refer back to the time of silence at beginning of the lesson. Ask students how they felt and what they thought of when they heard the opening questions.
6. Using a color not yet used, have students mark one or more adventures they have had.
7. Tell students to use another color to mark a special place and to note why that place is special.
8. Have students write a paragraph or two about something from their life in their own voice. You may want to encourage them not to write about something too personal.
9. Instruct students not to put their name on their papers. Collect and redistribute the papers. Based on voice, students can guess whose paper they have. If many know their classmates' handwriting, have them put their names on the papers and turn them in. Type the papers; leave the names off.

## Lesson Closing

Ask students if it was easy or difficult to recognize a classmate's writing by what they had written without having a name on the paper. Why or why not? What characteristics of voice did the author use that helped you, the reader, understand the "voice"?

# The Best Pet Ever

## Objective

Given an example of a personal letter displaying the characteristics of voice, the student will compose a persuasive letter to a friend or relative.

## Standards

- Standard 1E: Uses strategies to edit and publish written work (e.g., proofreads using a dictionary and other resources; edits for grammar, punctuation, capitalization, and spelling at a developmentally appropriate level; incorporates illustrations or photos; shares finished product)

- Standard 1H: Dictates or writes detailed descriptions of familiar persons, places, objects, or experiences

- Standard 1J: Writes in a variety of formats (e.g., picture books, letters, stories, poems, information pieces)

- Standard 2A: Uses general, frequently used words to convey basic ideas

- Standard 3: Uses grammatical and mechanical conventions in written compositions

## Materials

- paper for rough drafts (optional)

- stationery for final drafts (if available, use computer-generated stationery and offer a few different designs from which students can choose)

- stamps

- envelopes

- personal letter (one you personally have received) (optional)

- each student should bring an address for a friend or relative (written out)

## Lesson Opening

Say to students, "We all like to get mail. What is the best part about reading a letter?"

## Lesson Directions

1. Read selections from a personal letter that demonstrates qualities of the Voice Trait. Ask students to identify those characteristics as exemplified in the letter you just read.

2. Discuss how students might use characteristics of the Voice Trait in their own letter writing (e.g., being yourself; not trying to exaggerate or impress your reader; writing out of your own thoughts, feelings, and who you are; bringing your topic to life; etc.).

# The Best Pet Ever *(cont.)*

**Lesson Directions** *(cont.)*

3. Tell students they will be writing a persuasive letter. Explain that such a letter tries to convince the reader to believe or act in a certain way. In their letter, they should write to convince the reader that a llama would be a good pet.

4. Have students think of a real person to whom they would like to write. You may wish to have them write their persuasive letters to you or another staff member. Remind them to use the qualities just discussed as they write. Depending on your class, you might want them to write a rough draft first before they write a final copy on stationery. Have students edit their writing for proper capitalization, punctuation, and spelling. This will also allow the teacher to check student writing for voice. You may also need to give your students some questions to get them started in their thinking.

5. Have students write a final copy of their letter on stationery and prepare it for mailing. Assist students in addressing the envelope, using the printed address they brought from home.

6. Collect letters for mailing. (See if parents will volunteer postage or if there is money for postage from the parent-teacher organization.)

## Lesson Closing

Ask students if they felt using the characteristics of the Voice Trait made their letter easier and more interesting to read and write. Why? Would they like to receive such a letter? Why or why not?

## Extension Activity

Have students write a personal (rather than persuasive) letter to a friend or relative.

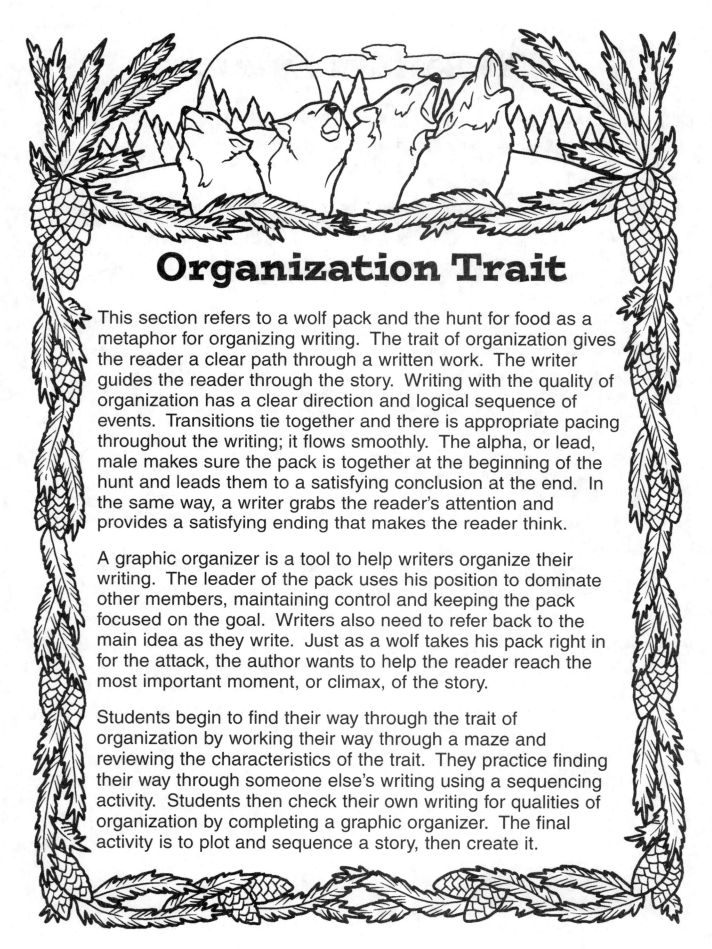

# Organization Trait

This section refers to a wolf pack and the hunt for food as a metaphor for organizing writing. The trait of organization gives the reader a clear path through a written work. The writer guides the reader through the story. Writing with the quality of organization has a clear direction and logical sequence of events. Transitions tie together and there is appropriate pacing throughout the writing; it flows smoothly. The alpha, or lead, male makes sure the pack is together at the beginning of the hunt and leads them to a satisfying conclusion at the end. In the same way, a writer grabs the reader's attention and provides a satisfying ending that makes the reader think.

A graphic organizer is a tool to help writers organize their writing. The leader of the pack uses his position to dominate other members, maintaining control and keeping the pack focused on the goal. Writers also need to refer back to the main idea as they write. Just as a wolf takes his pack right in for the attack, the author wants to help the reader reach the most important moment, or climax, of the story.

Students begin to find their way through the trait of organization by working their way through a maze and reviewing the characteristics of the trait. They practice finding their way through someone else's writing using a sequencing activity. Students then check their own writing for qualities of organization by completing a graphic organizer. The final activity is to plot and sequence a story, then create it.

# Tracking the Wolves

**Objective** ·
Given the characteristics of the Organization Trait, the student will become familiar with the qualities of organization by completing a maze worksheet.

**Standards**
- Standard 1A: Uses prewriting strategies to plan written work (e.g., discusses ideas with peers, draws pictures to generate ideas, writes key thoughts and questions, rehearses ideas, records reactions and observations)
- Standard 1B: Uses graphic organizers, story maps, and webs; groups related ideas; takes notes; brainstorms ideas.

**Materials**
- "Tracking the Wolves" (page 52)
- wolf pattern (page 53)
- red yarn, cut into 24" (61 cm) pieces

**Preparation**
Enlarge two copies of the wolf pattern for classroom display. Program one poster with the characteristics of the Organization Trait. Program the second poster with the following:

- guided by the leader
- alpha male in the lead
- logical order of events during the hunt
- wolves can adapt to habitats
- coordinated for the hunt
- satisfied at end of hunt
- wolves run long distances
- sharp teeth

Reproduce one copy of page 52 onto an overhead transparency and one paper copy per student.

**Lesson Opening**
Ask students if they know how a wolf pack hunts and catches prey. You may also ask the following:

- How does the pack find prey? (*The pack is guided by the leader.*)
- How do wolves attack their prey? (*Wolves follow a logical sequence of events.*)
- What happens at the end of the hunt? (*The wolves eat and are satisfied; they may celebrate success.*)

**Lesson Directions**
1. Introduce the concept(s) of the Organization Trait using the analogy of a wolf pack.
2. Teach the trait of organization. Tell students that writing with this trait has the following:

   - path leading the reader to main point
   - clear direction and purpose
   - an attention-getting introduction
   - conclusion that makes the reader think
   - logical order and sequencing of details
   - appropriate pacing
   - transitions that tie together
   - links back to the main idea

3. Refer to the wolf posters. Ask students to match the first trait of the Organization Trait to a characteristic of a wolf pack as listed on the second poster. Attach red yarn to the two posters to match the characteristics.
4. Distribute page 52 and have students complete the maze. If they finish early, they may design a maze for a partner and write in trait qualities around it.

**Lesson Closing**
Ask, "How will the wolf pack help you remember the characteristics of the Organization Trait?"

# Tracking the Wolves *(cont.)*

Start

End

# Wolf Pattern

# He Huffed, and He Puffed, and...

## Objective

Given a read-aloud experience, the student will identify events from the story and put them in proper sequence.

## Standards

- Standard 1A: Uses prewriting strategies to plan written work (e.g., discusses ideas with peers, draws pictures to generate ideas, writes key thoughts and questions, rehearses ideas, records reactions and observations)
- Standard 1G: Dictates or writes with a logical sequence of events (e.g., includes a beginning, middle, and ending)
- Standard 1I: Writes in response to literature

## Materials

- copy of *The Three Little Wolves and the Big Bad Pig* by Eugene Trivizas
- index cards, 6 per student
- "Following the Pack" (page 55)
- colored pencils

## Lesson Opening

Tell students they will hear a story read aloud. Ask them to listen to how the author organizes his story.

## Lesson Directions

1. Read *The Three Little Wolves and the Big Bad Pig* aloud to the class. (See Bibliography on page 92 for book information.)
2. Lead a classroom discussion about the story's organization based on the previously taught characteristics.
3. Distribute six index cards to each student. Have them write one event or scene from the story on each card. Ask them not to number the cards. When they have completed the task, students are to swap their set of cards with a partner. Each student will then put his or her partner's cards in the proper sequence. Have them number the cards with a colored pencil.
4. Tell students to give the cards back to their partner. Have the original student number his or her cards with a different color pencil. Ask students if it was easy or hard to put their partner's cards in order, and why.
5. Distribute page 55 and use it as further organization practice.

## Lesson Closing

Ask students, "Are you beginning to understand how an author organizes a story? What do you notice about the beginning and the ending of the story?

# Following the Pack

**Directions:** On a separate piece of paper, copy the sentences below in an order that makes sense.

1. They close upon the prey silently, isolating one deer from its herd.

2. Hunting in a group enables them to catch larger prey.

3. The wolves bite the deer repeatedly until it becomes weak from loss of blood and finally dies.

4. The alpha male takes the lead, with the rest of the pack following single file.

5. After they eat and are satisfied, the pack may howl to celebrate a successful hunt.

6. The wolves use a system of sounds and body movements to communicate and launch a surprise attack.

7. He guides his pack through their territory.

--------------------------------------------------------------------------
*(Fold the page under before making copies so that the answer key does not show.)*

### ———————————————— Answer Key ————————————————

1. The alpha male takes the lead, with the rest of the pack following single file.

2. He guides his pack through their territory.

3. Hunting in a group enables them to catch larger prey.

4. The wolves use a system of sounds and body movements to communicate and launch a surprise attack.

5. They close upon the prey silently, isolating one deer from its herd.

6. The wolves bite the deer repeatedly until it becomes weak from loss of blood and finally dies.

7. After they eat and are satisfied, the pack may howl to celebrate a successful hunt.

# Alpha and Omega

## Objective

Given sample leads and conclusions from literature, the student will identify what makes them effective by discussing as a class. The student will then identify effective beginnings and endings using resources from the classroom library. Finally, the student will write his/her own sample leads and conclusions.

## Standards

- Standard 2: Develops awareness of the stylistic and rhetorical aspects of writing
- Standard 2C: Uses a variety of sentence structures

## Materials

- "Alpha and Omega" (page 57)

## Preparation

Reproduce page 57 on overhead transparencies.

## Lesson Opening

Read aloud two sample story beginnings, one effective, one ineffective. Ask students if they would want to read the first story or the second. Why?

## Lesson Directions

1. Review the Organization Trait. Remind students that two of the characteristics of organized writing are a beginning that grabs the reader's attention and a satisfying ending.

2. Ask students what kind of story beginning makes them want to keep reading. How might an author get the reader's attention? Brainstorm these qualities as a class and list them on the board or overhead. Include concepts from the Organization Trait in the discussion.

3. Read aloud and/or display on an overhead story beginnings and endings from literature (page 57) and discuss.

4. Tell students they will work with a partner to find effective beginnings and endings. Have students look through books in the classroom library and write down examples of two opening sentences and two closing sentences.

5. Ask students to write one sample lead and one sample conclusion of their own. Collect student papers. (You may wish to evaluate and make comments as necessary.)

## Lesson Closing

Ask students what they have learned about writing beginnings and endings for their stories. Ask them what makes this part of writing easy or difficult.

# Alpha and Omega *(cont.)*

**Directions:** Discuss the following story beginnings and endings from literature.

## Beginnings

1. "The night Max wore his wolf suit and made mischief of one kind and another his mother called him 'Wild Thing!' and Max said 'I'll eat you up!' so he was sent to bed without eating anything." (*Where the Wild Things Are*. Maurice Sendak. Harper Collins, 1963.)

2. "One day something arrived in a brown paper bag for James." (*Something for James*. Shirley Isherwood. Dial Books for Young Readers, 1995.)

3. "This story happened a long time ago, way back when the animals could still talk around these parts." (*The Three Little Pigs and the Fox, an Appalachian Tale*. William H. Hooks. Aladdin, 1989.)

4. "The plane from Mexico was landing." (*Soccer Sam*. Jean Marzollo. Random House, 1987.)

5. "'Archie, look what I found,' Peter shouted through the pipe." (*Goggles!* Ezra Jack Keats. Aladdin, 1969.)

## Endings

1. "Something gave a happy sigh as he snuggled down under the blanket. One of his soft gray paws was still a little damp." (*Something for James*. Shirley Isherwood. Dial Books for Young Readers, 1995.)

2. "But if you think Anansi learned his lesson, you're mistaken. Because he's still playing tricks to this very day." (*Anansi and the Moss-Covered Rock*. retold by Eric A. Kimmel. Holiday House, 1988.)

3. "That's it. The real story. I was framed. But maybe you could loan me a cup of sugar." (*The True Story of the 3 Little Pigs, by A. Wolf*. "As told to" Jon Scieszka. Scholastic, 1989.)

4. "And if you ever hear Coyote's voice, way out in the desert at night… well, you know what he's remembering!" (*The Three Little Javelinas*. Susan Lowell. Scholastic, 1992.)

5. "'Yeah, I suppose, if you're the kind of kid who likes class trips to the farm.'" (*The Day Jimmy's Boa Ate the Wash*. Trinka Hakes. Noble Dial Press, 1980.)

# On the Hunt

## Objective

Given a graphic organizer, the student will complete it using a sample of his or her actual writing.

## Standards

- Standard 1A: Uses prewriting strategies to plan written work (e.g., discusses ideas with peers, draws pictures to generate ideas, writes key thoughts and questions, rehearses ideas, records reactions and observations)
- Standard 1B: Uses graphic organizers, story maps, and webs; groups related ideas; takes notes; brainstorms ideas
- Standard 1C: Uses strategies to draft and revise written work (e.g., rereads; rearranges words, sentences, and paragraphs to improve or clarify meaning; varies sentence type; adds descriptive words and details; deletes extraneous information; incorporates suggestions from peers and teachers; sharpens the focus)
- Standard 1D: Elaborates on a central idea, uses paragraphs to develop separate ideas
- Standard 1F: Evaluates own and others writing (e.g., asks questions and makes comments about writing, helps classmates apply grammatical and mechanical conventions)

## Materials

- student-generated rough drafts from previous assignments (e.g., "Bear Ideas")
- "On the Hunt" (page 59)
- wolf patterns on display

## Preparation

Reproduce page 59 on an overhead transparency and reproduce one or two copies for each student.

## Lesson Opening

Discuss with the class the logical sequence of events of a hunt.

## Lesson Directions

1. Briefly review the characteristics of the Organization Trait. Ask students, "Would a reader be able to make sense of your writing?" Tell students if their writing has the trait of organization, a reader will not get lost. There will be clear direction, and the writing will make sense.
2. Distribute student writing folders and/or rough drafts. Ask students to look through their writing to find a story idea about which they would like to write.
3. Display page 59 on the overhead and distribute copies. Explain each item on the page.
4. Have students complete the graphic organizer, using elements from their rough drafts.
5. Ask students to add or make changes to their graphic organizer as needed. Explain that these changes will help them in writing their story.
6. When students write their stories, remind them to use complete sentences. Tell them they might not actually use what they wrote for "purpose," but it will help them stay focused on the main idea. Remind them to use other traits (e.g., word choice, fluency, and voice) in their writing.

## Lesson Closing

Ask, "How did this exercise help you to organize your thoughts and your story. What kinds of changes did you need to make? Did using the graphic organizer make it easier to write the stories? Why?"

# On the Hunt *(cont.)*

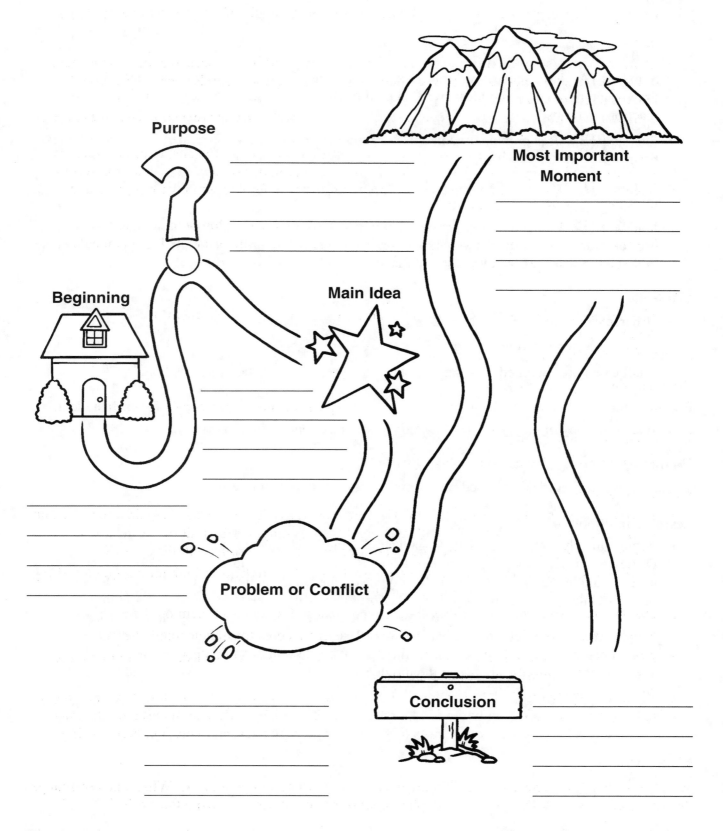

**Purpose**

**Most Important Moment**

**Beginning**

**Main Idea**

**Problem or Conflict**

**Conclusion**

# A Character's Adventures

## Objective

Given a simple story model, the student will plot out and write a story using a graphic organizer.

## Standards

- Standard 1A: Uses prewriting strategies to plan written work (e.g., discusses ideas with peers, draws pictures to generate ideas, writes key thoughts and questions, rehearses ideas, records reactions and observations)

- Standard 1B: Uses graphic organizers, story maps, and webs; groups related ideas; takes notes; brainstorms ideas

- Standard 1J: Writes in a variety of formats (e.g., picture books, letters, stories, poems, information pieces)

- Standard 1K: Writes expressive composition (e.g., expresses ideas, reflections, and observations; uses an individual, authentic voice; uses relevant details; and presents ideas that enable a reader to imagine the world of the event or experience)

## Materials

- "Character's Adventures" (page 62)

- "The Character's Journey" (page 63)

- small cards programmed with sample characters, settings, conflicts, etc. (optional)

## Preparation

Reproduce one copy of page 62 for each student and make one overhead transparency.

## Lesson Opening

Tell students many stories are based on a simple, basic model of storytelling.

## Lesson Directions

1. Review the characteristics of the Organization Trait. Ask students to think about their favorite Disney movies and/or classic stories such as *Pinnochio*. Ask students, "What does every story need?" Guide the discussion to include types of characters, actions, or events, the steps in the process as the hero tries to solve his or her problem or meet a challenge set before him or her. Have them think about how the stories end. Do they always have a happy ending? List each story element on the board as it is discussed. Use the story outline on page 62, if needed, to prompt discussion. Ask students how the current discussion ties in with the trait of organization. What are the similarities between the movie/story outline as discussed in class and the characteristics of the trait?

# A Character's Adventures *(cont.)*

**Lesson Directions** *(cont.)*

2. Explain the concept of a "storyboard": an author or scriptwriter often plots out the events of a story and arranges them in a logical order.

3. Tell the class to set aside thoughts of their favorite movie/story. If you wish, have students select pre-programmed story element cards. Display "The Character's Journey" (page 63) on the overhead. Lead a discussion, going through the page one item at a time, using examples (e.g., a story about a class arriving to find a substitute teacher for the day).

4. Distribute copies of page 63. Have students plot out a story. Encourage them to make up their own characters, events, etc. If you choose to use pre-programmed cards, have students select one or more character cards, setting cards, and a conflict card. Have them use these cards to get ideas as they plan a story.

5. Students should then write out the story, using complete sentences.

## Lesson Closing

Ask students how organizing the pieces of the story first helped them in their writing. You might want to have students retain their stories to use as rough drafts further in the writing process through Conventions (editing) and Presentation (publishing).

# A Character's Adventures *(cont.)*

## ─────── Story Outline Questions ───────

☆ What types of characters are in the story? Are there good characters or bad characters? Is the hero or heroine perfect or flawed?

☆ What are the patterns in the story?

☆ What does your main character want? What problems does he or she encounter? What steps will he or she take to solve the problem(s)?

☆ Does anyone help or hinder the main character along the way?

☆ Is there any danger?

☆ What role does the "bad guy" play?

☆ How does the character overcome the difficulty?

☆ How does the story end? Does it always end "happily ever after"?

☆ Does the hero or heroine reach the desired goal? Why or why not? Is there more than one part to the conclusion?

# The Character's Journey

1. The main character, or hero, is in his or her ordinary world.

2. The hero is asked to leave his/her comfort zone; this day will not be ordinary. He/she is presented with a problem or challenge, something he/she has to solve, perhaps something he/she must obtain.

3. The hero doesn't want to do the task. There may also be a fear of the unknown.

4. Someone comes along and gives the hero advice, encouragement, or tools he or she will need. The hero must still solve the problem on his or her own. The help may come from a person or it may come from something the hero reads.

5. The adventure begins for the hero. He or she is required to be in a new setting and may not be sure how to get there.

6. The main character faces various problems. How will the hero react under stress? What tests and other obstacles will he or she face?

7. Obstacles grow more difficult; the hero finds himself in trouble, in a dangerous place (physical or otherwise).

8. The hero tries many things, none of which seems to work. He or she faces the end of his options and struggles for survival.

9. The hero solves the problem. He or she now has met the challenge, obtained the prize.

10. As the main character faced obstacles, there may have been consequences. The hero must now deal with these consequences.

11. The character faces one last obstacle or ordeal. Your hero must survive this one as well. This need not be a happy ending, but it must make sense and be satisfactory.

12. The hero returns to his or her ordinary world, with the problem solved. He or she may also bring back whatever he obtained on the journey (new knowledge, prize, etc.).

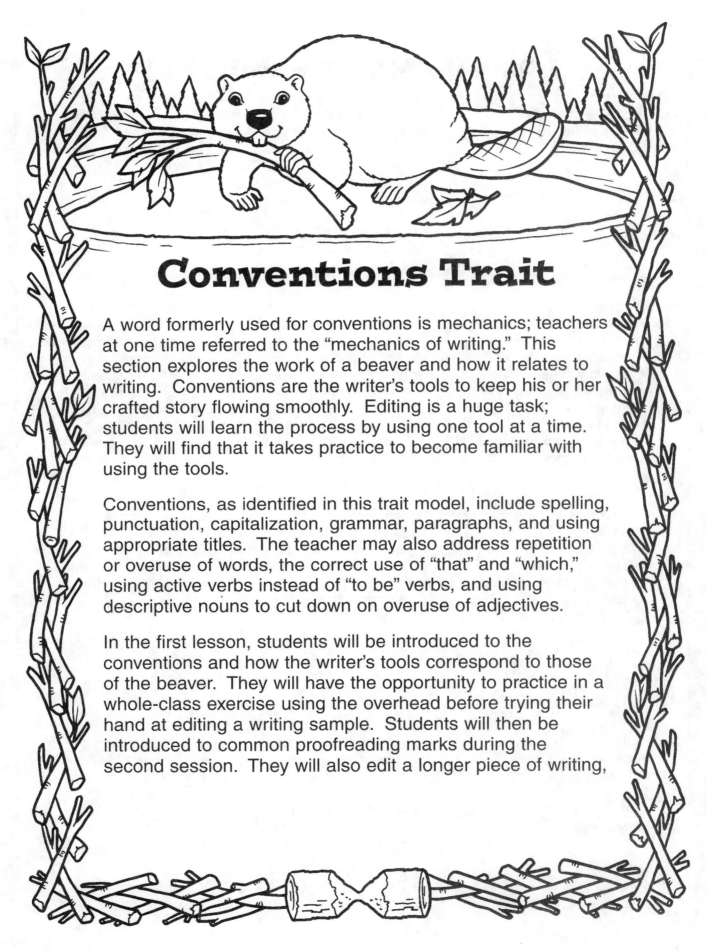

# Conventions Trait

A word formerly used for conventions is mechanics; teachers at one time referred to the "mechanics of writing." This section explores the work of a beaver and how it relates to writing. Conventions are the writer's tools to keep his or her crafted story flowing smoothly. Editing is a huge task; students will learn the process by using one tool at a time. They will find that it takes practice to become familiar with using the tools.

Conventions, as identified in this trait model, include spelling, punctuation, capitalization, grammar, paragraphs, and using appropriate titles. The teacher may also address repetition or overuse of words, the correct use of "that" and "which," using active verbs instead of "to be" verbs, and using descriptive nouns to cut down on overuse of adjectives.

In the first lesson, students will be introduced to the conventions and how the writer's tools correspond to those of the beaver. They will have the opportunity to practice in a whole-class exercise using the overhead before trying their hand at editing a writing sample. Students will then be introduced to common proofreading marks during the second session. They will also edit a longer piece of writing,

# Beaver Tools

## Objective
Given an overview of the Conventions Trait, the student will write a short piece and edit it.

## Standards
- Standard 1E: Uses strategies to edit and publish written work (e.g., proofreads using a dictionary and other resources, edits for grammar, punctuation, capitalization, and spelling at a developmentally appropriate level)
- Standard 1F: Evaluates own and others' writing
- Standard 3: Uses grammatical and mechanical conventions in written compositions

## Materials
- beaver pattern for classroom display (page 67)
- "A Beaver's Tools" (page 68)
- tape or sticky fabric dots
- "Editing Practice" (page 69)
- picture book about beavers (optional)

## Preparation
Reproduce "A Beaver's Tools" and "Editing Practice" onto overhead transparencies.

## Lesson Opening
Tell students that although they will be hearing about the Conventions Trait, conventions at one time were known as mechanics and teachers used to refer to the "mechanics of writing." Tell students that writers need tools to correct their writing. Ask students, "Which animals have tools?"

## Lesson Directions
1. Read aloud the picture book about beavers and/or discuss beavers with the class. Brainstorm with the students the tools a beaver uses (teeth, tail, paws, nose, claws, etc.). List these on the board.
2. Teach the trait. Tell students that to edit means to use the tools of a writer to correct a piece of writing, including the following:

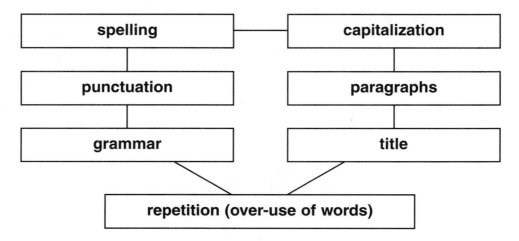

# Beaver Tools *(cont.)*

## Lesson Directions *(cont.)*

3. Write each of the writing conventions next to one of the beaver "tools" listed on the board. Tell students these will be the tools they will use to work on their writing.

4. Show the first sample of writing that needs to be edited (page 69). Ask students what needs to be corrected and what tools should be used to do so (e.g., capitals—teeth, periods—tail, spelling—claws). As students state each convention, show the class the appropriate body-part tag and have student volunteers use tape or sticky fabric dots to attach the tag to the appropriate part of the beaver pattern on classroom display.

5. Ask students if they want to add other tools from the lesson to the beaver on display that haven't already been posted.

6. Ask students to write a paragraph about beavers, based on the read-aloud experience.

7. Read aloud each convention, slowly. Have students look over their papers for obvious corrections that need to be made. Have them draw a circle around the error to be corrected.

8. Collect the papers for later use.

## Lesson Closing

Ask students, "What do we mean when we talk about conventions?" (*We mean tools we use to correct our writing, or the "mechanics" of writing*.) "Which will be the hardest for you to remember to use in your own writing? Which will be the easiest?"

# Beaver Pattern

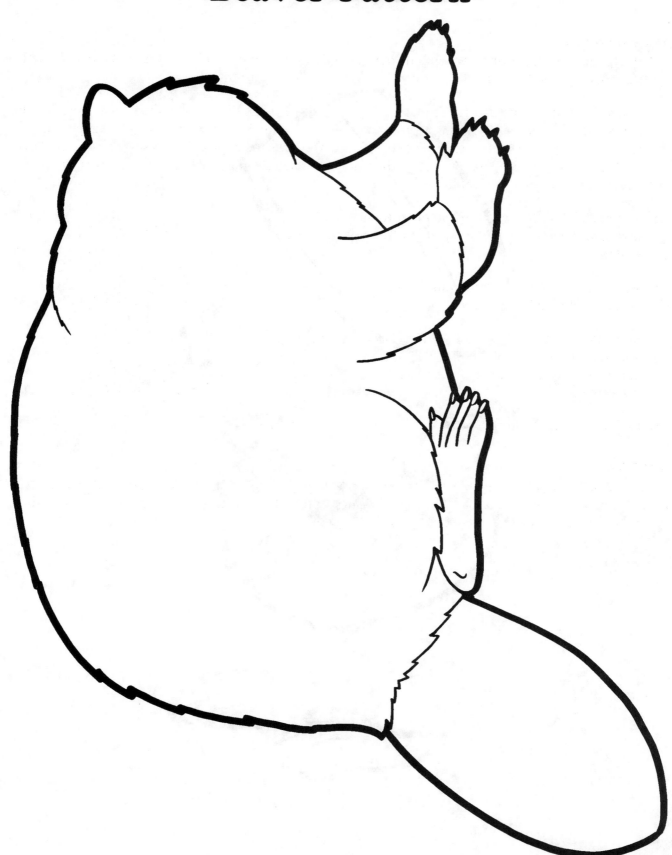

# A Beaver's Tools

# Editing Practice

### Paragraph #1 (13 corrections)

Bevers have tails that they use to swim.  There teeth is the most importim part of them Femals have the babes.

Bevers bild dens to sleap in.  There fat cep them warm.  they have paws to protect them.

—Sara Greer (*used with author's permission*)

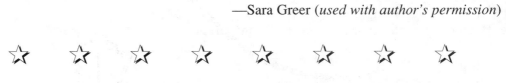

### Paragraph #2 (10 corrections)

A beavers tail is flat Beavers can grow anuther eye layer.  Beavers nose is inportin.  a beavers teeth is very sharp.  Beavers build lodhes.  Beavers have a layer of fat to keep them warm.

—Trey Udy (*used with author's permission*)

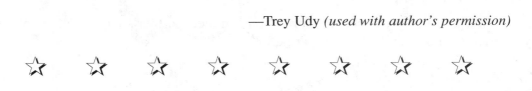

### Paragraph #3 (13 corrections)

Beavers are like mechanics.  they have everything  They need to bild a dam's.  I thingk beavers hold ther breth for a long time.  beavers have tools. And good wons to.

—Taylor Briscoeray (*used with author's permission*)

# From One Beaver to Another

## Objective
Given sentences, the student will write the sentences correctly using the conventions.

## Standards
- Standard 1F: Evaluates own and others' writing (e.g., asks questions and makes comments about writing, helps classmates apply grammatical and mechanical conventions)
- Standard 3: Uses grammatical and mechanical conventions in written compositions

## Materials
- "From One Beaver to Another" (page 71)
- colored pencils

## Preparation
Copy page 71 onto chart paper or an overhead transparency.

## Lesson Opening
Tell students they will begin learning about the editing process by practicing using some of the conventions.

## Lesson Directions
1. Display "From One Beaver to Another."
2. Have students write the sentences. Remind them to use correct spelling, capitalization, punctuation, and grammar.
3. Have students swap papers with a partner. Go over corrections together as a class, using the overhead or chart paper.
4. Ask students to make any necessary corrections on their partner's paper with a colored pencil. Have students return papers to their partner.

## Lesson Closing
Ask students what they learned about editing today. Ask, "Which conventions did you have the most trouble remembering to use?"

# From One Beaver to Another *(cont.)*

## Editing Practice

1. A beaver (chew/chews) a snack of bark and twigs.

2. beavers build dams lodges and canals

3. Beavers (has/have) sharp strong teeth to cut down trees.

4. kathy heard a beaver slap its tail

5. did the beavers dam flood johns farm

- - - - - - - - - - - - - - - - - - - - - - - - - - - - - - - - - - - - - - - - - - - - - - - - - -

*(Fold the page under before making copies so that the answer key does not show.)*

## Answer Key

1. A beaver chews a snack of bark and twigs.

2. Beavers build dams, lodges, and canals.

3. Beavers have sharp, strong teeth to cut down trees.

4. Kathy heard a beaver slap its tail.

5. Did the beaver's dam flood John's farm?

# Busy Beaver

## Objective

Given a writing sample, the student will practice editing for conventions, focusing on one element at a time.

## Standards

- Standard 1E: Uses strategies to edit written work (e.g., edits for grammar, punctuation, capitalization, and spelling at a developmentally appropriate level; considers page format [paragraphs, indentations, titles])
- Standard 1F: Evaluates others' writing
- Standard 3: Uses grammatical and mechanical conventions in written composition

## Materials

- beaver pattern on classroom display
- "Common Proofreading Marks" (page 73)
- "Busy Beaver's Homework" (page 74), one copy per student
- colored pencils

## Preparation

Reproduce one copy of page 74 onto an overhead and reproduce one paper copy for each student. Reproduce page 73 onto an overhead.

## Lesson Opening

Draw the students' attention to the beaver display created in the previous lesson. Ask if a beaver uses all of his tools at once, or one at a time. Explain to the students that they will practice using the conventions one at a time by editing "Busy Beaver's Homework."

## Lesson Directions

1. Review the conventions poster.
2. Teach the proofreader's marks (page 73). Display the overhead and write in the appropriate symbol as you discuss each one. Explain that these will be the students' editing "tools."
3. Display additional sample paragraphs(s) ("Editing Practice," page 69) on the overhead one at a time. Model and discuss how to edit using the proofreading marks.
4. Distribute page 74 and display the overhead. Ask students to use a colored pencil to edit the sample. Have them circle misspelled words and write the correct version above it. Discuss the difference between spelling errors and grammatical errors (for example, a word that is spelled correctly but used incorrectly in a sentence would be considered a grammatical error).
5. Next, have students edit for punctuation, using a different color pencil than the one used in step 4. Remind them to use the "Common Proofreading Marks" format.
6. Continue with grammar, capitalization, and marking paragraphs. Conclude by creating a title.

## Lesson Closing

Ask the class how it felt to practice using the tools one at a time. To review the tools, point to the beaver parts one at a time and ask students to name a convention to look for in editing.

# Common Proofreading Marks

| Editor's Mark | Meaning | Example |
|---|---|---|
| ≡ | capitalize | they fished in lake tahoe |
| / | make it lower case | Five $tudents missed the Bus. |
| sp. | spelling mistake | The day was clowdy and cold. |
| ⊙ | add a period | Tomorrow is a holiday⊙ |
| ⸜ | delete (remove) | One person knew the the answer. |
| ∧ | add a word | Six were in the litter. |
| ⸝ | add a comma | He planted peas corn, and squash. |
| ∾ | reverse words or letters | An otter swam in the bed kelp. |
| ∨ | add an apostrophe | The childs bike was red. |
| ⸜⸝ | add quotation marks | Why can't I go? she cried. |
| # | make a space | He ate two redapples. |
| ◡ | close the space | Her favorite game is soft ball. |
| ¶ | begin a new paragraph | to know. Next on the list |

# Busy Beaver's Homework

I works hard during spring break.  my family built a neew lodge.

First, we built a dam to mak the pond deeper then dad chewed down

some trees with his strong sharp teeth.  I used my front paws to

carry large branches to the water.

We always worked together so that one of us culd watch for danger If

an enemy came close, I would slapped my tail on the water to warn

the others.  Mabe the animal would get frightened and go away.  Did

you know that beavers are great

engineers I had a grat time

helping my family build during

spring break.

# Beaver Life

## Objective

Given writing samples and cue cards, the student will practice editing for conventions, focusing on one element at a time.

## Standards

- Standard 1E: Uses strategies to edit written work (e.g., edits for grammar, punctuation, capitalization, and spelling at a developmentally appropriate level; considers page format [paragraphs, indentations, titles])
- Standard 1F: Evaluates others' writing
- Standard 3: Uses grammatical and mechanical conventions in written compositions

## Materials

- "A Beaver's Tools" (page 68)
- colored pencils
- writing sample (pages 76–77)
- beaver pattern on classroom display

## Preparation

Photocopy two sets of beaver cue cards on page 68. Enlarge if necessary. Cut the cards apart. You may wish to create a packet using pages 76–77 for each student for ease in completing the "assembly line" exercise (see #3, below).

## Lesson Opening

Draw the students' attention to the beaver display created in a previous lesson. Ask if a beaver uses all of his "tools" at once, or one at a time. Explain to the students that they will learn to use the conventions one at a time in editing.

## Lesson Directions

1. Review the conventions poster and proofreading marks.
2. Divide the class into six groups.
3. Explain the following "assembly line" activity: each group starts with a cue card and the corresponding writing sample. Use only three cue cards the first day—i.e., two groups will have a spelling card, two groups will have a capitals card, two groups will have a punctuation card. Students will edit for the remaining conventions during a second work period. Give students time to edit the appropriate sample, correcting only the convention represented by that cue card. At the end of the work period, each group passes the cue card to the next group, and everyone turns to the appropriate page. You may wish to have students use colored pencils, preferably in the same color as the card, to edit. Direct students to do some of the work individually and some as a group.

## Lesson Closing

Ask the class how it felt to practice using the tools one at a time. Ask students to review the tools by holding the cue cards one at a time and asking students to name a convention to look for when editing.

# Writing Sample

**Directions:** Edit the following writing sample.

**Spelling:** Find 6 spelling errors. Write the word correctly above the incorrectly spelled word.

"Oh no! Not agin! Randy, get back here now!" As usal, Randy the beaver didn't lisen.

"What am I going to do with him?" said Randy's mom. Away from his mother, Randy slowed down and stared to look for his friend Shanzea.

"Shanzea!" He called. "Shanzea!"

"Yeah?" said Shanzea, the wolf.

"Let's go and explor the marsh," said Shanzea.

"Nah, how abot the fox's lair?" Randy asked.

**Capitalization:** Find 7 errors. Use the proofreading marks to make corrections.

Only a year before, randy had gotten lost and had almost been eaten by the fox, Rontu. Shanzea had saved Randy in the nick of time. ever since, they had been best friends.

"There he is," said Randy.

The beaver and the Wolf were outside the fox's lair, well hidden in some bushes. Rontu called a meeting of the council. he had fought his way up and was now head of the pack.

"Whom should We attack?"

Ramsea spoke up. "As female head of the pack, I vote to attack the beavers' lodge."

"Excellent idea. paws up for attacking the beavers' lodge. Anyone against? The

**Punctuation:** Find 6 punctuation errors. Use the marks to make corrections.

"Help Help Mom and Dad! Foxes are planning to attack our dam!"

"Randy, quit trying to scare us and get to work"

"Now! Shanzea, go home. Randy cant play anymore. He has to help repair the dam."

"Mom, I'm not joking."

"You're grounded" his mother said firmly.

The next day Randy pretended to be sick. When his mother's back was turned, Randy was out of the dam and running. His mother called after him, but Randy paid no attention. He found Shanzea waiting for him in the woods.

# Writing Sample *(cont.)*

**Grammar:** Find 8 grammar errors. Circle the error and write the word(s) correctly above the incorrect word(s).

"I has an idea, Shanzea said.

"What?"

"We could trick them. When they come to the dame, well get their attention and hopefully they'll chase us. We'll head them to the waterfall and put a rotten logs over the top of it. They'll try to cross but the log will break!"

"How are we going to get across?" ask Randy.

"We will cross one at a time so there won't be enough weight to break it."

"Good idea! Lets find pinecones to throw at them and make them mad, to."

"Ok!" says Shanzea.

They goes to work. Then, they quietly snuck back to the fox's lair to see if they could learn anything else about the plan of attack.

"There's no one here," said Randy. "Let's go back."

**Paragraphs:** Find 4 paragraph breaks and show them using proofreader's marks.

The next morning, the foxes attacked. "Let's go!" said Rontu. The whole pack chased Randy and Shanzea. The two friends raced up to the waterfall. They had agreed to let Randy go first. If need be, Shanzea could fight the foxes until Randy got safely across. When they got to the bridge, Randy raced across. Shanzea waited until Randy made it to the other side, then he started out. When he was halfway, the foxes ran on to the log. Just before the bridge collapsed, Shanzea jumped clear. All of the foxes fell down the waterfall and died. Exhausted, Randy and Shanzea finally reached the beaver dam. "You were wonderful!" exclaimed Randy's mom. Randy's mom hugged an embarrassed Shanzea. "You were great, too." "Awww..." said Shanzea. After the celebration, Randy never disobeyed his mother again. Well, almost never.

**Title:** Write a title for the story.

—*sample used with permission of author Kenneth Mabry.*

# Beaver Work

## Objective

Given a review of conventions, the student will edit a fellow student's work one step at a time, becoming more familiar with editing in the process.

## Standards

- Standard 1E: Uses strategies to edit written work (e.g., edits for grammar, punctuation, capitalization, and spelling at a developmentally appropriate level, considers page format [paragraphs, margins, indentations, titles])
- Standard 1F: Evaluates others' writing
- Standard 3: Uses grammatical and mechanical conventions in written composition

## Materials

- beaver pattern on classroom display
- student-generated rough draft paragraphs from "Beaver Tools" lesson
- colored pencils or red pencils
- dictionaries, student spelling books, or other spelling aids

## Preparation

Remove student names from rough draft paragraphs. If handwriting is easily identifiable, enlist volunteer aid to type the paragraphs.

## Lesson Opening

Tell students they will continue to practice editing by correcting a fellow student's work.

## Lesson Directions

1. Discuss with students how sometimes it's difficult to remember all the conventions when editing, or correcting, our work.
2. Review the beaver poster on display, and also go over proofreading marks with students.
3. Have students edit one convention at a time, using colors that correspond to the colors of the cue cards that you created for the lesson (page 68). Ask students to use the same color of pencil to edit their work in the same manner. Model editing on the board or overhead, if necessary.
4. Have the class begin with spelling. Continue with punctuation, grammar, capitalization, and marking paragraphs. Conclude with creating titles.
5. Collect papers and return them to the original authors. If time allows, you may wish to have students rewrite their paragraph as a final (edited) copy.

## Lesson Closing

Ask students if editing is becoming easier by focusing on one convention at a time.

## Extension Activity

Distribute student-generated rough drafts from Bear Ideas or other previous lessons. Review the steps in the writing process. Encourage students to edit their work, using colors and editing for only one convention at a time.

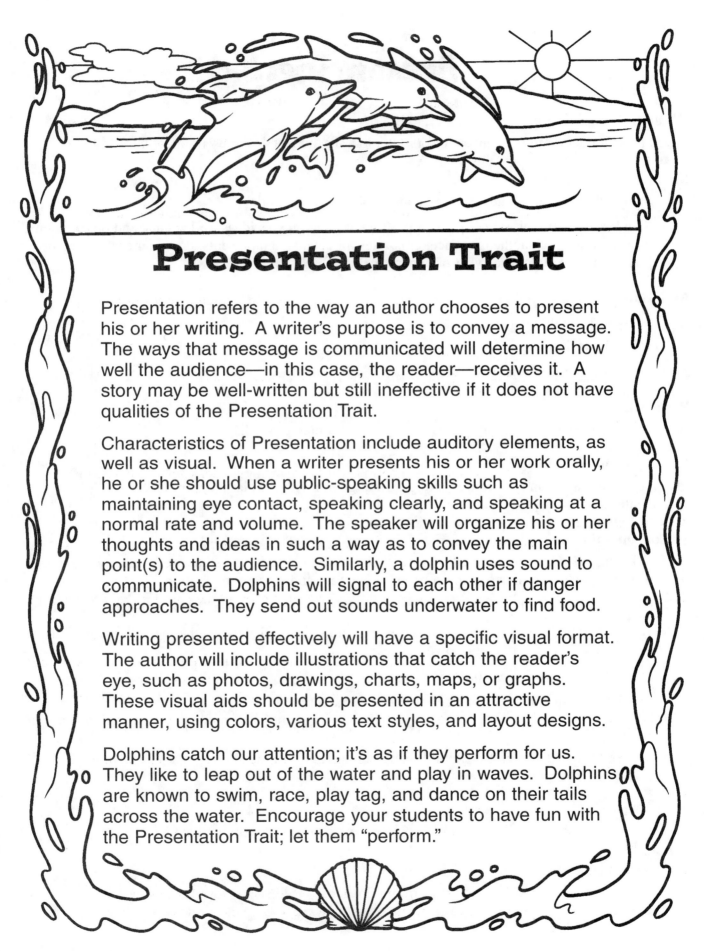

# Presentation Trait

Presentation refers to the way an author chooses to present his or her writing. A writer's purpose is to convey a message. The ways that message is communicated will determine how well the audience—in this case, the reader—receives it. A story may be well-written but still ineffective if it does not have qualities of the Presentation Trait.

Characteristics of Presentation include auditory elements, as well as visual. When a writer presents his or her work orally, he or she should use public-speaking skills such as maintaining eye contact, speaking clearly, and speaking at a normal rate and volume. The speaker will organize his or her thoughts and ideas in such a way as to convey the main point(s) to the audience. Similarly, a dolphin uses sound to communicate. Dolphins will signal to each other if danger approaches. They send out sounds underwater to find food.

Writing presented effectively will have a specific visual format. The author will include illustrations that catch the reader's eye, such as photos, drawings, charts, maps, or graphs. These visual aids should be presented in an attractive manner, using colors, various text styles, and layout designs.

Dolphins catch our attention; it's as if they perform for us. They like to leap out of the water and play in waves. Dolphins are known to swim, race, play tag, and dance on their tails across the water. Encourage your students to have fun with the Presentation Trait; let them "perform."

# Presenting...

## Objective

Given an introduction to the concept of presentation, the student will present his or her name.

## Standards

- Standard 1E: Uses strategies to edit and publish written work

- Standard 1K: Writes expressive composition (e.g., expresses ideas, reflections, and observations; uses an individual, authentic voice; uses relevant details; and presents ideas that enable a reader to imagine the world of the event or experience)

## Materials

- white construction paper

- colored pencils

- dolphin pattern for classroom display, page 82 (optional)

## Preparation

Enlarge two copies of the dolphin pattern, if desired, for classroom display.

## Lesson Opening

Play a game of hangman (or similar word guessing game) with the class to introduce the word "presentation."

## Lesson Directions

1. Ask students what it means to "present" their writing. You may wish to use "feature presentation" from the cinema to illustrate the concept of auditory and visual presentation.

2. Discuss dolphins with the class. Explain that dolphins display visual and auditory cues to others.

3. Teach the trait. Begin by reviewing visual presentation. Tell students that when presenting their writing, they should do the following:

   - select a presentation format

   - include illustrations that catch the reader's attention

   - incorporate various visual aids (such as photos, drawings, charts, and graphs)

   - express their own ideas and reflections.

# **Presenting...** *(cont.)*

**Lesson Directions** *(cont.)*

4. Tell the class that presentation includes auditory as well as visual elements. Teach students that oral presentation includes the following:

   - telling about personal experiences and/or personal knowledge about a topic

   - asking and responding to questions

   - having a clear main point when speaking to others

   - reading their writing to the class

   - making eye contact while giving oral presentations

   - organizing ideas for oral presentations (e.g., includes content appropriate to the audience, uses notes or other memory aids, summarizes main points).

5. You may wish to list the visual and auditory characteristics of presentation on two dolphin posters for classroom display.

6. Ask students how authors present their writing. List ideas on the board—books, movies, speeches, telling stories, decorations (walls, clothes), letters, graphic art, etc.

7. Distribute a piece of construction paper to each student. Tell the class they will be "presenting" their names. Encourage students to be creative with their lettering style and use of color.

## **Lesson Closing**

Display the completed name posters around the room. Ask students how each poster reflects the personality of the person who created it.

## **Extension Activities**

Have students write a paragraph about themselves, titled "I Am…," or "Presenting [their name]." Display the paragraphs anonymously around the room, and invite students to guess which student wrote each piece. If computer stations are available, have students design a screen saver using their name. Use the "Scrolling Marquee" screen saver option in Windows. (/My Computer/Control Panel/Display/Screen Saver)

# Dolphin Pattern

# Nature Presents...

## Objective

Given an outdoor experience, the student will write observations of the world around himself or herself and relate those observations to the Presentation Trait.

## Standards

- Standard 1H: Dictates or writes detailed descriptions of familiar persons, places, objects, or experiences
- Standard 1K: Writes expressive composition (e.g., expresses ideas, reflections, and observations; uses an individual, authentic voice; uses relevant details; and presents ideas that enable a reader to imagine the world of the event or experience)
- Standard 5C: Reads compositions to the class

## Materials

- clipboard, one per student (clipboards can be made from binder clips and 8¹/₂" x 11" (22 cm x 28 cm) pieces of cardboard)
- plain white paper
- colored pencils

## Preparation

If clipboards are not available, attach binder clips to the edges of pieces of cardboard to create them.

## Lesson Opening

Ask students how nature presents itself. Student responses may include flowers, trees, clouds. Direct their thoughts to include various types of weather.

## Lesson Directions

1. Briefly review characteristics of the Presentation Trait. Tell the class that, as authors, we present our writing so others can see and hear our ideas.
2. Discuss how weather is a visual and auditory presentation.
3. Distribute clipboards to the class. Have them put a piece of paper on the clipboard. (You may wish to remind students to keep the clips in place.)
4. Take the class outside for a weather walk in the schoolyard. Have students write their observations of the weather and other elements of nature. (If the weather is too inclement for the weather walk, have students gather around windows and observe from there.)
5. Following the walk, have students refer to their observations to design a presentation.
6. Distribute paper to each student. Direct the class to title their page (e.g., "Presenting…").
7. Allow students to share their work if time allows. You may wish to remind them of the oral characteristics of presentation (e.g., making eye contact).

## Lesson Closing

Ask students what they learned about presentation by observing nature. You may wish to add student input to the classroom posters on display at this time.

## Extension Activity

Show the class a dolphin or ocean video, if available. Discuss characteristics of the trait as presented in the film.

# Dolphin Talk

## Objective

Given guided practice in the steps of writing a speech, the student will present his or her ideas orally to the class.

## Standards

- Standard 1A: Prewriting: Uses prewriting strategies to plan written work. (e.g., discusses ideas with peers, draws pictures to generate ideas, writes key thoughts and questions, rehearses ideas, records reactions and observations)

- Standard 5: Demonstrates competence in speaking and listening as tools for learning

## Materials

- index cards, 5 per student
- visual-aid samples (page 86)
- plain white paper
- colored pencils

## Preparation

Reproduce the visual-aid samples (page 86) onto overhead transparencies.

## Lesson Opening

Direct students' attention back to the illustration of cinema. Tell them today they will focus on the auditory aspect(s) of presentation by giving a speech.

## Lesson Directions

1. Review the auditory characteristics of the Presentation Trait.

2. Introduce the concept of writing a speech. Tell students that the best speeches are written before speaking. Teach students the steps in writing a speech. Tell them they will need to choose a topic, have at least three main points (things they wish to say about that topic), and include a visual aid.

3. Display the overhead transparency samples to illustrate the use of visual aids in giving a speech. Say that an effective visual aid is something that gives information about or helps to further explain the topic.

# Dolphin Talk *(cont.)*

**Lesson Directions** *(cont.)*

4. Discuss with students possible topics. They should plan to talk about a familiar subject. If necessary, suggest the following sample topics:

   - sports
   - animals or pets
   - cars
   - school

   - science topics
   - other specific topics studied (e.g., pioneers)
   - activities and/or hobbies (e.g., hiking)

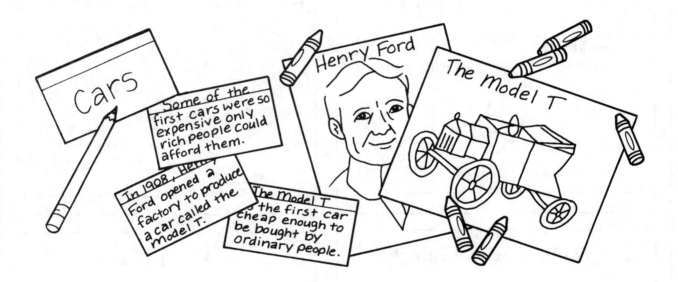

5. Distribute index cards. Have students select a topic, and write that topic on one card.

6. Next, ask students to think of three things they would like to say about that topic. Have them write one thing on each of the three remaining index cards. Encourage the class to write other notes about each of their three main points to use as reminders when speaking to the class.

7. Ask students to consider what type of visual aid would enhance their speech. On the fifth card, students should write their choice of visual aid. Have the class set aside their index cards.

8. Distribute white paper. Allow time for students to design and create a visual aid. Visual aids may be as simple or elaborate as you wish.

9. Have students present their speeches.

**Lesson Closing**

Ask students what qualities made the speeches they heard effective. You may wish to evaluate student speeches by scoring volume, rate, eye contact, content, and visual aid (for a total of 10 points).

# Visual-Aid Samples

## Presidents on U.S. Coins

Abraham
Lincoln

Thomas
Jefferson

Franklin D.
Roosevelt

George
Washington

John F. Kennedy

## How to Pitch a Baseball

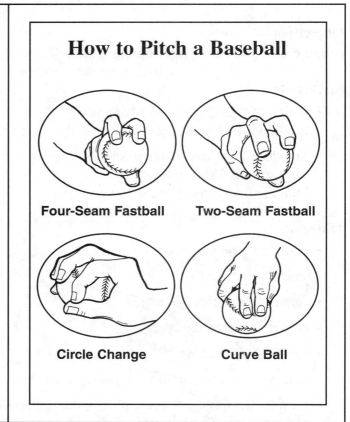

Four-Seam Fastball    Two-Seam Fastball

Circle Change    Curve Ball

## Most Popular School Lunches

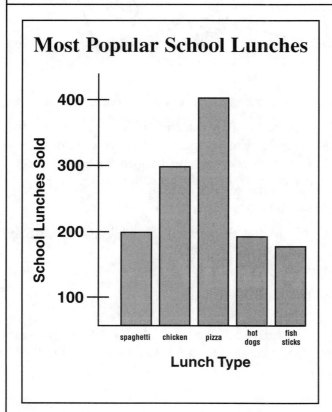

School Lunches Sold

400
300
200
100

spaghetti  chicken  pizza  hot dogs  fish sticks

**Lunch Type**

## All About Sharks

➤ Sharks have very keen vision.

➤ Sharks have skin that feels like sandpaper.

➤ Great White sharks are a protected species.

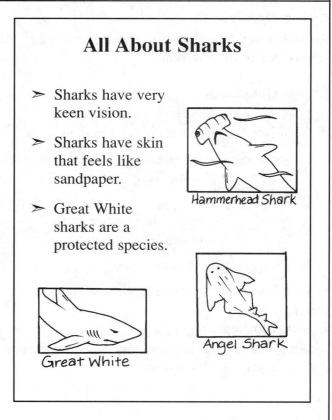

Hammerhead Shark

Great White

Angel Shark

# Creating a Presentation

**Objective**

Given various materials, the student will create a visual presentation of his or her writing.

**Standards**

- Standard 1E: Editing and Publishing: Uses strategies to edit and publish written work (e.g., incorporates illustrations or photos, shares finished product)

- Standard 1K: Writes expressive composition (e.g., expresses ideas, reflections, and observations; uses an individual, authentic voice; uses relevant details; and presents ideas that enable a reader to imagine the world of the event or experience)

**Materials**

- craft scissors with decorative cutting blades

- shape templates

- rulers with decorative edges

- colored construction paper

- stickers, if available

- magazine and newspaper advertisements (optional)

- sample "scrapbook" pages, if available (optional)

**Lesson Opening**

Review presentation, specifically the visual aspects. Tell students they will be visually presenting a short piece of their writing.

**Lesson Directions**

1. Have students write a short paragraph about a favorite animal. Their writing should be in a finished, neat format for use in their presentation.

2. Show sample scrapbook pages or advertisements. Introduce the concepts of graphic layout and design. Emphasize the use of color, letter style, and placement of text and illustrations on the page.

3. Tell the class they will incorporate their written paragraph into a "scrapbook" page. Discuss the materials available for use; model if necessary.

4. Give students time to create a visual page, guiding their work as needed.

5. Allow time for students to present their completed pages to the class.

**Lesson Closing**

Ask students what made various presentations effective. Incorporate qualities of the Presentation Trait into the discussion as applicable.

# What a Show

## Objective

Given a rough draft, samples of final copies, and the characteristics of the Presentation Trait, the student will publish a final copy of his/her writing.

## Standards

- Standard 1:  Demonstrates competence in the general skills and strategies of the writing process

- Standard 1E:  Editing and Publishing: Uses strategies to edit and publish written work (e.g., proofreads using a dictionary and other resources; edits for grammar, punctuation, capitalization, and spelling at a developmentally appropriate level; incorporates illustrations or photos; shares finished product)

- Standard 1F:  Evaluates own and others' writing (e.g., asks questions and makes comments about writing, helps classmates apply grammatical and mechanical conventions)

- Standard 1J:  Writes in a variety of formats (e.g., picture books, letters, stories, poems, information pieces)

- Standard 2:  Develops awareness of the stylistic and rhetorical aspects of writing

- Standard 3:  Uses grammatical and mechanical conventions in written compositions

- Standard 5C:  Reads compositions to the class

- Standard 5D:  Organizes ideas for oral presentations (e.g., includes content appropriate to the audience, uses notes or other memory aids, summarizes main points)

## Materials

- samples of student-published work—stories (bound with staples or bindings), folder stories, presentation boards, booklets, brochures, etc.

- construction paper, markers, colored pencils, glue, tagboard, and/or similar art supplies

## Lesson Opening

Ask students again how writing may be presented.  Encourage the class to brainstorm many different forms of presentation (e.g., advertising).

# What a Show *(cont.)*

## Lesson Directions

1. Display the samples. Ask students what elements make the presentation of the writing samples effective. Discuss such features as color, title, font style, illustrations, graphics, layout of the page, type of the presentation and/or binding, etc.

2. List options for presentation on the board. Have students select how they want to present their writing.

3. Distribute rough drafts and/or final copies of student work, e.g., stories from Bear Ideas or other writing assignment from a previous lesson. You may wish to review the steps in the writing process at this point. Allow time for students to work on the final written copy, if necessary.

4. Students will then design and create a final published format for their written work. These may then be presented to the class as time allows.

## Lesson Closing

Ask students how it feels to have completed a piece of writing from start to finish. Are they more satisfied, more pleased with the final copy than they were with the rough draft? Why? Is the process worth the work?

## Extension Activity

Give students the option of creating a multimedia presentation, if computer or other resources are available. Options might include video cameras and other recording devices, or the use of computer software programs such as *Kid Pix* and *PowerPoint*.

# On Safari

## Objective

Given a specific time, the student will invite family and friends to view and experience student work created during the study of the traits.

## Standards

- Standard 4C: Compiles information into oral reports.
- Standard 5: Demonstrates competence in speaking and listening as tools for learning
- Standard 5A: Makes contributions in class and group discussions (e.g., recounts personal experiences, reports on personal knowledge about a topic, initiates conversations
- Standard 5B: Asks and responds to questions
- Standard 5D: Organizes ideas for oral presentations (e.g., includes content appropriate to the audience, uses notes or other memory aids, summarizes main points)

## Materials

- white construction paper (optional)
- markers, colored pencils, and/or crayons (optional)
- bulletin board space for display(s) of student work
- student work and/or folders created during the trait writing unit

## Preparation

Prepare bulletin board display space for student work. Decorate with a jungle theme, if possible. You may wish to use titles from some of the lessons taught (e.g., "It's a (Wild) Day in the Jungle").

## Lesson Opening

Tell students, "We've been living in the jungle with the traits now for several weeks. Let's invite your family and friends to join us on our safari."

## Lesson Directions

1. Review the traits, using any classroom posters on display. Ask students to create an invitation for a parent, family member, or friend, inviting the person(s) to an Open House. List the date, time, and other pertinent information on the board for students to copy.

2. Enlist student help to decorate the classroom for the Open House. Follow a jungle/safari theme as much or as little as you would like. Display student work. (You may wish to group assignments around the room by trait, using the poster displays.)

3. In addition, you may wish to encourage some students to prepare a short oral presentation, introducing the traits studied.

4. Allow time at the Open House for students to give oral presentations as well.

## Lesson Closing

Say, "Now that we've become more familiar with each trait, hopefully it will be easier to include these qualities in our writing. Which trait is easiest for you to use in your own writing? Why? Which is the most difficult? What have you learned that will help you develop those characteristics in your writing?" Give positive feedback by citing examples of how the class has put these traits into practice.

# Technology Resources

***Microsoft Publisher '97.***   Microsoft Corporation.
  ➤ desktop-publishing program.

The program enables students to incorporate original text with clip art to create their own publications.

***Microsoft Word '97*** *(or later version).*   Microsoft Corporation.
  ➤ word-processing program

Word also allows students to add clip art to their documents.  It is easy to enter text and edit.  The "insert comment" and "auto correct" features allow teachers to disable automatic corrections of common student errors and to edit and comment on student work.

***ClarisWorks***
  ➤ integrated-task program

An all-in-one application that includes word processing, spreadsheet, database, painting, and graphics modules.  It also includes an extensive clip art library and several templates to help with common writing tasks.  This program is available for both PC and MacIntosh computers (but is most often used with MacIntosh).

***Storybook Weaver Deluxe.***   MEDCC/The Learning Company (1994)
  ➤ writing program, ages 6–12

Pictures and sounds provide story starters for students to create their own stories.  Stories may be written and edited within the program.  Students may also hear their story read aloud back to them.

***Student Writing Center.***   The Learning Company
  ➤ desktop-publishing program

Program includes five document types, writing process and grammar tips for students, and teacher's lesson ideas and worksheet templates.

***Kid Pix.***   The Learning Company.
  ➤ a paint, draw, and graphics program

---

### Internet Web Sites

**Merriam-Webster Online**
  ➤ *http://www.m-w.com*
This site features an online dictionary and thesaurus.

**edHelper.com**
  ➤ *http://www.edhelper.com*
This site has word puzzles and worksheets covering a variety of themes.

**Teachers.Net**
  ➤ *http://www.teachers.net*
A valuable resource for teachers, this site includes many language arts lesson plans.

---

# Bibliography

────────────── **Fiction** ──────────────

Aardema, Verna. *Anansi Finds a Fool*. Dial Books for Young Readers, 1992.

Guarne, Deborah. *My Mama is a Llama*. Scholastic, 1989.

Hakes, Trinka. *The Day Jimmy's Boa Ate the Wash*. Noble Dial Press, 1980.

Hooks, William H. *The Three Little Pigs and the Fox, an Appalachian Tale*. Aladdin, 1989.

Isherwood, Shirley. *Something for James*. Dial Books for Young Readers, 1995.

Keats, Ezra Jack. *Goggles!* Aladdin, 1969.

Kimmel, Eric A., retold by. *Anansi and the Moss-Covered Rock*. Holiday House, 1988.

Kimmel, Eric A, retold by. *Anansi Goes Fishing*. House, 1992.

Lowell, Susan. *The Three Little Javelinas*. Scholastic, 1992.

Marzollo, Jean. *Soccer Sam*. Random House, 1987.

Minarik, Else Holmelund. *Little Bear*. Harper and Row, 1957.

Rey, H. A. *Curious George Gets a Job*. Houghton Mifflin, 1957, 1985.

Scieszka, Jon. *The True Story of the 3 Little Pigs, by A. Wolf, as told to*. Scholastic, 1989.

Sendak, Maurice. *Where the Wild Things Are*. HarperCollins, 1963.

Shine, Michael. *Mama Llama's Pajamas*. Romar Books, 1990.

Trivizas, Eugene. *The Three Little Wolves and the Big Bad Pig*. Scholastic, 1993.

# Bibliography *(cont.)*

━━━━━━━━━━━━━━━━━━ **Nonfiction** ━━━━━━━━━━━━━━━━━━

Arnold, Caroline. *Llama.* Morrow Junior Books, 1988.

Bailey, Donna. *Bears.* Steck-Vaughn, 1991.

Banks, Martin. *Polar Bear on Ice.* Gareth Stevens Publishing, 1989.

Benson, Robert. *The Life of Prayer and the Art of Writing.* Retreat, 1998.

Betz, Dieter. *The Bear Family.* Tambourine Books, 1991.

Ericson, Anton. *Whales & Dolphins.* Kidsbooks, 1994.

Goodall, Jane. *Chimps.* Macmillan Publishing Company, 1989.

Grasey, John. *Eyes on Nature: Apes and Monkeys.* Kidsbooks, 1997.

Hodge, Deborah. *Beavers.* Kids Can Press, 1998.

Hoffman, Mary. *Bear: Animals in the Wild.* Scholastic, 1986.

Julivert, Maria Angels. *The Fascinating World of Wolves.* Barron's, 1996.

LaBonte, Gail. *The Llama.* Dillon Press, Macmillan Publishing Company, 1988.

Lane, Margaret. *The Beaver.* Dial Books for Young Readers, 1981.

Larsen, Thor. *The Polar Bear Family Book.* Verlog Neugebaure Press, Picture Book Studio, 1990.

Lepthien, Emilie. *Llamas.* Children's Press, Grolier Publishing, 1996.

Matthews, Downs. *Polar Bear Cubs.* Simon and Schuster, 1989.

Podendorf, Illa. *Spiders.* Children's Press, 1982.

Resnick, Jane P. *Eyes on Nature: Spiders.* Kidsbooks, 1996.

————. *Eyes on Nature: Wolves and Coyotes.* Kidsbooks, 1995.

Ryden, Hope. *The Beaver.* G. P. Putnam's Sons, 1986.

Smith, Roland. *Whales, Dolphins, and Porpoises in the Zoo.* Millbrook Press, 1994.

Steedman, Scott. *Amazing Monkeys.* Alfred A. Knopf, 1991.

Wexo, John Bonnett. *Bears.* Zoo Books, 1997.

Wooldridge, Susan G. *poemcrazy.* Clarkson Potter, 1996.

# Answer Key

## Page 46

Voices are from the following individuals. Your students will present a wide variety of answers. Accept reasonable responses.

1. 8-year-old male, student (permission granted by Taylor Briscoeray, May 2002)
2. 8-year-old female, student (permission granted by Brianna Kalita, May 2002)
3. 13-year-old male, student (permission granted by Brian Mabry, May 2002)
4. 61-year-old female, retired librarian (permission granted by Helen Lantis, April 2000)
5. 43-year-old male, house painter (permission granted by Dennis Blackwell, April 2000)
6. young adult female, student (Tracie Heskett)

(**Note to the teacher:** You may wish to copy the corrected paragraphs that follow onto overheads to display to students for correcting their own work, or you may make regular paper copies to give to students for the same purpose.)

## Page 52—Tracking the Wolves

## Page 69—Editing Practice

**Paragraph #1** (*13 corrections*)
Beavers have tails that they use to swim. Their teeth are the most important part of them. Females have the babies.

Beavers build dens to sleep in. Their fat keeps them warm. They have paws to protect them.

**Paragraph #2** (*11 corrections*)
A beaver's tail is flat. Beavers can grow another eye layer. A beaver's nose is important. A beaver's teeth are very sharp. Beavers build lodges. Beavers have a layer of fat to keep them warm.

**Paragraph #3** (*13 corrections*)
Beavers are like mechanics. They have everything they need to build a dam. I think beavers hold their breath for a long time. Beavers have tools, and good ones, too.

## Page 74—Busy Beaver's Homework

(*13 corrections*)
I work hard during spring break. My family built a new lodge. First, we built a dam to make the pond deeper. Then dad chewed down some trees with his strong, sharp teeth. I used my front paws to carry large branches to the water.

We always worked together so that one of us could watch for danger. If an enemy came close, I would slap my tail on the water to warn the others. Maybe the animal would get frightened and go away. Did you know that beavers are great engineers? I had a great time helping my family build during spring break.

# Answer Key *(cont.)*

**Pages 76 and 77—Writing Samples**

**Spelling** (*6 errors*)

"Oh no!  Not again!  Randy get back here now!"

As usual, Randy the beaver didn't listen.

"What am I going to do with him?" said Randy's mom.

Away from his mother, Randy slowed down and started to look for his friend Shanzea.

"Shanzea!" he called, "Shanzea!"

"Yeah?" said Shanzea, the wolf.

"Let's go and explore the marsh," said Shanzea.

"Nah, how about the fox's lair?" Randy asked.

**Capitalization** (*7 errors*)

Only a year before, Randy had gotten lost and had almost been eaten by the fox, Rontu.  Shanzea had saved Randy in the nick of time.  Ever since, they had been best friends.

"There he is," said Randy.

The beaver and the wolf were now just outside the fox's lair, well hidden in some bushes.  Rontu called a meeting of the council.  He had fought his way up and was now head of the pack.

"Whom should we attack?"

Ramsea spoke up.  "As female head of the pack, I vote to attack the beavers' lodge."

"Excellent idea.  Paws up for attacking the beavers' lodge.  Anyone against?  The vote:  yes, 15; no, 0. We will attack in two days.  Be ready," said Rontu.

**Punctuation** (*6 errors*)

"Help!  Help!  Mom and Dad!  Foxes are planning to attack our dam!"

"Randy, quit trying to scare us and get to work."

"But. . ."

"Now! Shanzea, go home.  Randy can't play anymore.  He has to help repair the dam."

"Mom, I'm not joking."

"You're grounded," his mother said firmly.

The next day Randy pretended to be sick.  When his mother's back was turned, Randy was out of the dam and running.

He found Shanzea waiting for him in the woods.

# Answer Key *(cont.)*

**Pages 76 and 77** *(cont.)*

**Grammar** (*7 errors*)

"I have an idea," Shanzea said.

"What?"

"We could trick them. When they come to the dam, we'll get their attention and hopefully they'll chase us. We'll head them to the waterfall and put a rotten log over the top of it. They'll try to cross but the log will break!"

"How are we going to get across?" asked Randy.

"We will cross one at a time so there won't be enough weight to break it."

"Good idea! Let's find pinecones to throw at them and make them mad, too."

"Ok!" said Shanzea.

They went to work. Then, they quietly snuck back to the fox's lair to see if they could learn anything else about he plan of attack.

"There's no one here," said Randy. "Let's go back."

**Paragraphs** (*4 errors*)

The next morning, the foxes attacked.

"Let's go!" said Shanzea.

The whole pack chased Randy and Shanzea. The two friends raced up to the waterfall.

They had agreed to let Randy go first. If need be, Shanzea could fight the foxes until Randy got safely across.

When they got to the bridge, Randy raced across. Shanzea waited until Randy made it to the other side, then he started out. When he was halfway, the foxes ran on to the log. Just before the bridge collapsed, Shanzea jumped clear. All of the foxes fell down the waterfall and died.

Exhausted, Randy and Shanzea finally reached the beaver dam.

"You were wonderful!" exclaimed Randy's mom.

"Thanks."

Randy's mom hugged an embarrassed Shanzea. "You were great, too."

"Awww…," said Shanzea.

After the celebration, Randy never disobeyed his mother again. Well, almost never.